The Poetic Fiction of José Lezama Lima

The Poetic Fiction
of **José Lezama Lima**

Raymond D. Souza

University of Missouri Press
Columbia, 1983

Copyright © 1983 by
The Curators of the University of Missouri
University of Missouri Press
Columbia, Missouri 65211
Library of Congress Catalog Card Number 83–1056
Printed and bound in the United States of America

Library of Congress Cataloging in Publication Data

Souza, Raymond D., 1936–
    The poetic fiction of José Lezama Lima.

    Bibliography: p.
    Includes index.
    1. Lezama Lima, José—Criticism and
interpretation.
I. Title.
PQ7389.L49Z86   1983   861   83–1056
ISBN 0–8262–0406–6

The production of this book was partially
financed by the Frank Luther Mott Fund.

For Richard and Robert

Preface

I am indebted to many individuals and groups for direct and indirect help in the preparation of this manuscript. I wish to thank the Center for Humanistic Studies at the University of Kansas for a stimulating faculty seminar on semiotics, the University of Kansas General Research Fund for summer grants, my colleagues in the Department of Spanish and Portuguese for an open, but not uncritical, forum for the exchange of ideas, and the Exxon Foundation and the University of Kansas College of Liberal Arts and Sciences for making possible a year's leave to pursue studies in philosophy and linguistics. Special thanks are due John Brushwood, Michael Doudoroff, and Luz María Umpierre for their patient reading of this manuscript.

For the benefit of non-Spanish-speaking readers, translations of Spanish quotations have been included in an appendix. They have been numbered to correspond to the numbers following the quotations in the text, for easy cross-reference. Acceptable English versions of Lezama Lima's works were used when available and are identified in the footnotes and the bibliography. Unidentified translations are my own. Anyone familiar with Lezama Lima can appreciate the difficulties involved in translating his writings. I consider my own translations as only crude approximations of the originals. Since the few quotations that appear in the footnotes are for specialists who may wish to pursue a particular line of research, I have not translated them.

R. D. S.
Lawrence, Kansas
April 1983

Contents

Introduction

Shortly after the appearance of the novel *Paradiso* in 1966, Julio Cortázar stated that the quality of José Lezama Lima's writings is equal to those of Jorge Luis Borges and Octavio Paz.[1] Nine years later Emir Rodríguez Monegal made an even more definitive statement: "Hoy, en América Latina, y en el mundo occidental, la obra de Lezama Lima ha sido reconocida como una de las decisivas de este siglo, y su nombre ha terminado por ser situado por su calidad e importancia junto al de Borges y el de Octavio Paz"[2] (A1). Lezama Lima's works undoubtedly form an important and major body of literature, and critical interest in his publications continues to grow. However, his challenging and innovative writings require patient reading if one is to fully enjoy their aesthetic qualities. International fame and recognition did not come to Lezama Lima until late in his career because of the hermetic nature of his works.

Lezama Lima's creative writings outstrip available critical methodologies. This partially accounts for the proclivity of some critics to rely on Lezama Lima's essays for explanations of his work and to see his creative endeavors as extensions of

1. Cortázar, "Para llegar a Lezama Lima." This article has been republished several times and is most readily available in his *La vuelta al día en ochenta mundos*. Cortázar further states:

> Me propongo solamente señalar una ignorancia vergonzosa y romper por adelantado una lanza contra los malentendidos que la seguirán cuando Latinoamérica oiga por fin la voz de José Lezama Lima. De la ignorancia no me asombro; también yo desconocía a Lezama doce años atrás, y fue preciso que Ricardo Vigón, en París, me hablara de *Oppiano Licario* que acababa de publicarse en *Orígenes* y que ahora cierra (si es que algo puede cerrarlo) *Paradiso*. Dudo de que en esos doce años la obra de Lezama haya alcanzado la presencia actual que en un plazo equivalente fueron logrando la de un Jorge Luis Borges o la de un Octavio Paz, a cuya altura está sin la más mínima duda. Razones de dificultad instrumental y esencial son una primera causa de esa ignorancia; leer a Lezama, es una de las tareas más arduas y con frecuencia más irritantes que puedan darse. (*La vuelta al día*, 136–37)

2. Rodríguez Monegal, "La nueva novela vista desde Cuba," 654.

his philosophical or aesthetic concepts. Severo Sarduy cautioned against this tendency: "No caer en la trampa de la crítica: un lenguaje mimético, una recreación del estilo—que se vuelve una recreación de los 'tics'—del autor. Evitar todo giro lezamesco"[3] (A2). I have kept this admonition in mind and have avoided making this study an exposition of Lezama Lima's hermeneutics and poetics. But the validity and importance of such contributions are recognized; quotations from the essays have been used to illuminate pertinent points.

During the last two decades many new approaches have been incorporated into the critical idiom under the labels of *structuralism*, *semiotics*, and *poststructuralism*. Some critics have embraced aspects of these new methodologies with the fervor of those who have found a new religion, while others see these systems and their terminology as embodiments of the dehumanization of art prophesied by José Ortega y Gasset. I do not regard these methodologies as infallible or as complete solutions to the formidable problems involved in critical analysis, but they do offer valuable insights and new ways of looking at literary creations. And they can be particularly fruitful when applied to the challenges presented by writers such as Lezama Lima.

Russian Formalism, New Criticism, and current studies in structuralism and semiotics have contributed in varying degrees to the development of literary theory in this century. Although there are a number of significant differences among these diverse methodologies, their proponents have in common some general assumptions that represent a new direction in literary studies. They all have attempted to systematize theory and analysis and have demonstrated an interest in the precise and consistent application of methodologies.

Another interesting aspect of the evolution of literary analysis in the present century has been the successive waves of interest in literature by groups outside of or on the margins of the discipline. Folklorists, mythologists, psychologists, anthropologists, linguists, and philosophers have used literature for different purposes and with varying degrees of success and

3. Sarduy, "Dispersión (Falsas notas / Homenaje a Lezama)," 67.

influence. Examples of this trend can be found in the works of Roman Jakobson, Joseph Campbell, Carl Jung, Claude Lévi-Strauss, and Jacques Derrida. Such endeavors have provoked alarm in some academic circles because this interest in literature has been regarded as intrusive or subversive. However, such interdisciplinary ventures have their positive aspects for they demonstrate the vitality and universal appeal of literature as well as the many elements that can be embedded in language. As verbal configurations, literary works are manifestations of the human imagination—its creation of particular visions of the world. Many disciplines have been attracted to creative writings because they contain systematized interpretations of reality as well as the aesthetic and structured communication of those views. Many fields share a preoccupation with the way language functions and concentrate on the specific mechanisms of communication or the meanings that are conveyed.

Contemporary critical methodologies have stressed the importance of taking into account the fact that the systems and communicative processes embodied in literary works are activated each time a reader confronts a text. The reader's participation, then, becomes an important component of the dynamic process of a work. Current criticism also has been concerned with the manner in which a writer moves from external references to the formation of a literary creation—with his or her transformation of the basic materials of a story into the text the reader sees. This interest in the processes involved in the writer's creation of a text and the reader's response to the finished work is as important as the concepts of system and communication. Different theorists and critics, of course, choose to emphasize diverse aspects of these elements in varying degrees of depth and detail, and the success or failure of any particular methodology depends, in the final analysis, as much on the talent of the critic as on the validity of the method.

The following study uses and modifies methods derived from discourse analysis and structuralist and semiotic criticism. Although I am indebted to a number of thinkers, the writings of Seymour Chatman, Umberto Eco, and Cesare Segre have had the greatest influence on my work. I have attempted to strike a reasonable balance between theory and analysis. Some explanation of methodology seemed in order, but I have tried to avoid lengthy theoretical discussions. The result of this effort is a text that decidedly emphasizes analysis.

Some of the terminology used in this study is my own. Expressions such as *time-bound* and *time-free* are self-explanatory within the contexts in which they appear. Others, such as *expansive elements* and *limiting elements*, need some clarification. Limiting elements are specific factors that enable the reader to construct a framework on which his or her comprehension of the text can subsequently be based. Implicit in this concept is a movement in the direction of specificity, clarity, and the accessibility of the text—in a sense, the known. Expansive elements, on the other hand, are those factors that stimulate the reader's imagination and move him toward speculation and ambiguity. The movement here is toward vagueness and obscurity—the mysterious or unknown. The movement between expansive and limiting elements generates tension because it is inherently contradictory; unity of text depends in part on this interaction. The placement of a textual element within this classification system is determined by the element's function in the passage in which it appears.

The first chapter of this study serves as an introduction to Lezama Lima's writings, with particular emphasis on his poetry. It includes an examination of the points of contact between his poetry and his prose fiction, and a look at the problems he faced in his effort to combine imagery and story. In the next four chapters I have examined various aspects of language, characterization, plot development, and narration in *Paradiso* in the context of the narrative's movement between poetry and fiction and the preoccupation with time in the novel. These chapters also contain a discussion of the continuous and discontinuous aspects of Lezama Lima's narratives and an exploration of his frequent use of a device that I term *combinatory opposition*, which can be seen in metaphors in which meaning moves simultaneously in two directions. The last chapter, which synthesizes the methods used in the previous chapters, focuses primarily on the posthumous novel *Oppiano Licario*. A summary of some of the major characteristics of Lezama Lima's art includes discussion of his avoidance of closure and his preoccupation with death and eternity, concerns that underlie much of his work.

1

The Poetic Vision

José Lezama Lima dedicated most of his artistic career to poetry and always considered himself a poet, but it was the publication of a novel that brought him international fame and recognition. When *Paradiso* appeared in 1966, it produced a major sensation in and outside of his native Cuba because of its unique artistry and its frank treatment of homosexuality. Only a few friends and literary critics were prepared for the novel's excellence, because they were familiar with Lezama Lima's poetic accomplishments and had seen the first five chapters of *Paradiso* in the journal *Orígenes* between 1949 and 1955.[1] In many respects, Lezama Lima's achievement of sudden international fame was similar to that of Gabriel García Márquez. While they both attracted considerable attention with a single work, bursting onto the international scene in a spectacular and surprising fashion, their previously published works had been of exceptional quality and had already marked their evolution toward the creation of masterpieces. Lezama Lima was aided indirectly by the revolution of 1959, which attracted considerable international attention to Cuban achievements in many fields of endeavor. Although the Cuban edition of *Paradiso* consisted of only four thousand copies and the novel produced at best an ambivalent reaction in Cuba's official government circles, word of its publication spread rapidly throughout the Spanish-speaking world. Julio Cortázar and Mario Vargas Llosa published several favorable articles immediately after the appearance of *Paradiso*, and these positive commentaries by authors well-known and esteemed outside of Cuba attracted considerable attention.[2] Another decisive

1. Cintio Vitier speaks of the importance of *Paradiso* eight years prior to its publication, in his *Lo cubano en la poesía*, 39.
2. For a listing of these articles, see Justo C. Ulloa, "Contribución a la bibliografía de y sobre José Lezama Lima," 142, 154.

influence was the role of *Mundo Nuevo* and its able editor Emir Rodríguez Monegal. This journal did much to stimulate interest in Lezama Lima's *Paradiso* and García Márquez's *Cien años de soledad (One Hundred Years of Solitude)*.

Paradiso was not published until several years after its inception. Lezama Lima may have delayed publication because of the novel's intimate exploration of sexuality; the novel did not appear until after the death of his mother. However, this biographical consideration does not totally explain the delay in publication; it took Lezama Lima several years to write the novel. He did not work on *Paradiso* consistently during the many years before its completion; he focused attention on other activities as he sporadically diverted energy and thought to the conception and elaboration of his masterpiece. These other activities included an aesthetic preoccupation with the similarities and differences between poetry and prose fiction, a concern which intrigued Lezama Lima throughout his career.

A survey of his published poetic works between 1945 and 1960 (*Aventuras sigilosas*, 1945; *La fijeza*, 1949; and *Dador*, 1960) reveals a decided trend toward long poems and thematic statements. Robyn Rothrock Lutz has pointed out that the twelve prose poems in *La fijeza*:

> tend to be primarily narrative (rather than lyrical or expository) with the episodes linked by a chronological but not logical thread. The images he uses in the prose poems are usually ones that also appear in [his earlier] poems, but the lack of repeated motifs and of extended metaphors within individual prose poems weakens their structural unity and impact.
>
> The prose poems are primarily of interest because the narrative techniques they display show up in later poems and because they break down many of the barriers between poetry and prose. We have seen how in *Aventuras sigilosas* and *La fijeza* Lezama Lima adapts elements frequently associated with fictional prose to his poetry: the emphasis on the speaker's role as a narrator or commentator, the welding of poems into larger units, the use of an entire story as a symbol, the dependence on framing and linking devices. The prose poems confirm the growing importance of plot narration in Lezama's poetry.[3]

3. Robyn Rothrock Lutz, "The Poetry of José Lezama Lima," 120. In addition to his preoccupation with the differences between poetry and fiction, Lezama Lima occasionally gave some attention to the essay, and some of these

The publication of these books coincides with the writing of *Paradiso*, and there is an overlapping in all these works of the techniques and concerns expressed in the two genres. This overlapping indicates that he was exploring the limitations of artistic expression and was attempting to synthesize certain aspects of the two genres. It is debatable whether Lezama Lima's attempts to overcome the distinctions between poetry and prose fiction were always successful, but they helped prepare the way for his first novel, his most famous publication.

The major issue he dealt with in his consideration of poetry and fiction was the problem of how to combine imagery and story. For Lezama Lima, imagery in general and metaphor in particular represented the highest form of knowledge, a written synthesis of the known and intuitively sensed, a kernel of truth based on a secret and harmonious whole. He perceived metaphor as a timeless entity, a vertical extension freed from the confines of logical development and the constraints of time and space. The novel, on the other hand, depends on the development of story lines and is an artistic creation in which time and space are of crucial importance. Lezama Lima was fascinated by the implications of chronological development, either as a clear component of a story or as an entity that could be overcome or fragmented. He undoubtedly felt that the presentation of cause-and-effect relationships offered a view of existence that could lead to an apprehension of totalities, and the possibility of attaining wholeness attracted him.

In most of his work, however, unity was more a goal than an achieved reality; for him the struggle to create difficult texts was more exhilarating than the achievement of intellectual understanding. But as completeness and comprehension became more important to him, he was intrigued by the possibility of constructing a unified view of existence, one in which all the disparate threads of life could come together in a meaningful whole. It was at this point that the novel attracted him as an artistic form.

writings contain narrative and poetic elements. The autobiographical essay "Confluencias" in *Las eras imaginarias* provides a good example of Lezama Lima's interest in incorporating aspects of other genres into the essay.

Lezama Lima read extensively, and he most likely was aware of Hegel's view that the philosophical consciousness of the modern world (that is, the European community contemporary to Hegel) represented a dialectical synthesis of the poetry of the ancient Greek world and the prose of the Roman world. In *The Philosophy of History,* Hegel, relating historicity to the existence of written texts, states that the poetry of the Greeks is spontaneous and not faithful to sources, while the prose of the Romans is bound by the workings of cause and effect. In Hegel's view, ancient Greek poetry is metaphorical; it is marked by a "freedom of Spirit" and is concerned with the "transmutation of the finite." Roman prose, on the other hand, is metonymical; it is "the *prose* of life" and is marked by a "self-consciousness of finiteness."[4] There are echoes of this kind of thought in Lezama Lima's essays in *Las eras imaginarias.* Although Hegel did not serve as a model, Lezama Lima must have found food for thought in Hegel's emphasis on the aesthetic factors of written texts, on the importance of the spiritual in historical change, and on the temporal implications of the synthesis of prose and poetry.

As he composed *Paradiso,* Lezama Lima was challenged to consider ways in which he might combine time-bound and time-free elements. In some instances, this involved moving entities back and forth between these classifications. Characters, for example, are time-bound as far as their physical existence is concerned, but when Lezama Lima passes to a consideration of their essence, they become time-free and are treated as metaphors. For this reason the Colonel in *Paradiso* and Licario in *Oppiano Licario* (Lezama Lima's second novel) reappear after their deaths in passages of unusual poetic beauty as the characteristics that marked them continue to exist. Lezama Lima sometimes attempted to move an entire narrative sequence or chapter into a time-free category. A good deal of *Paradiso* is an inquiry into origins, an exploration of family history, which depends on a chronological awareness of cause and effect. However, chapter 12, which is particularly enigmatic and far removed from the content of the rest of the

4. Georg Wilhelm Friedrich Hegel, *The Philosophy of History,* 288.

novel, was incorporated into *Paradiso* to defy and overcome the barriers of time and space. This chapter tests the reader's acceptance of the fictional world Lezama Lima has created and presents a challenge of the sort that delighted its author.

The artistic strategies that Lezama Lima used in order to divine and announce his perception of the world were based on his faith in the revelatory power of language. But his immense belief in the creative force of language was not able to fully protect Lezama Lima from doubt. Although he was also a man of great religious faith, declining health and separation from many members of his family during his last years plunged him into doubt and despair.

This evolution of feeling is reflected in his work. An ironical self-awareness, evident throughout his career, became more pronounced in his later publications. This irony was often manifested in self-referential terms, both in *Paradiso* and in *Oppiano Licario*, as well as in his poetry, particularly in his last volume of poetry, *Fragmentos a su imán*.

Lezama Lima's movement toward clarity in his poetry and fiction suggests that he was placing less emphasis on the quest for the obscure as an end in itself. This shift away from the hermetic as a self-sufficient goal is indicative of the growing intensity of his desire to understand death's meaning.

Not only did Lezama Lima's increasing doubt spur a change in his stylistic approach; but a symbolic shift occurred as well. In most of Lezama Lima's works, the unknown was a sign of the mysteries of life. But this changed as his career progressed; its presence in later works indicated death. Also, in much of his work, the family is a metaphor for unity; conversely, absence and separation, which occur more frequently in later works, are signs of death and the dispersal it represents.

Evidence of Lezama Lima's shift in emphasis and tone can be found in a comparison of two poems written during different periods of his career: "Rapsodia para el mulo" (rhapsody for the mule), which was first published in 1942, and "Los fragmentos de la noche" (fragments of night), which appeared in 1973.[5] The first work is an affirmation of faith with some

5. Lezama Lima, "Rapsodia para el mulo," *Nadie Parecía*, no. 1 (September

tinges of doubt, whereas the second is an expression of uncertainty and despair.

The anecdotal basis for "Rapsodia para el mulo" is the journey of a heavily laden mule into a ravine. However, this kernel of a story is not presented in a progressive or logical manner, but rather in a series of images that express the mule's worth and destiny. Metonymical images that are based on associations with the mule (eyes, skin, hooves, tendons) are central to the poem. The opening line focuses on his surefooted step. An enumeration of his qualities is accompanied by a sense of suffering and danger.

> CON qué seguro paso el mulo en el abismo
>
> Lento es el mulo. Su misión no siente.
> Su destino frente a la piedra, piedra que sangra
> creando la abierta risa en las granadas.
> Su piel rajada, pequeñísimo triunfo ya en lo oscuro,
> pequeñísimo fango de alas ciegas.
> La ceguera, el vidrio y el agua de tus ojos
> tienen la fuerza de un tendón oculto,
> y así los inmutables ojos recorriendo
> lo oscuro progresivo y fugitivo.
> El espacio de agua comprendido
> entre sus ojos y el abierto túnel,
> fija su centro que le faja
> como la carga de plomo necesaria
> que viene a caer como el sonido
> del mulo cayendo en el abismo.[6] (A3)

The image of the mule hurtling downward through space is an instance of combinatory opposition, a frequently used device in this poem. The mule journeys over crests and into ravines, and, as the poem closes, his fall into the abyss is countered by trees that extend upward from the ravine. This combination of upward and downward movement is reinforced by other oppositions such as crests and abysses, light

1942): 3–6; Lezama Lima, "Los fragmentos de la noche," *Eco* 26, no. 155 (1973): 308–10, and *El Urogallo* 4, nos. 21–22 (May–August 1973): 31–32.

6. Lezama Lima, "Rapsodia," in his *La fijeza,* 52. Subsequent quotes are from this volume. The poem is more readily available in the 1975 edition of *Poesía completa,* but there are some minor differences between the two versions. For example, the last line ends with "todo abismo" in *La fijeza* and "todo el abismo" in *Poesía completa.*

and darkness, and stone and water. The most striking example of a configuration of opposites is the symbol of the cross, which appears when the speaker directly addresses the mule, and which refers to life and death as well as materiality and spirituality. These combinatory oppositions suggest that reality is more complicated and contradictory than it appears, and that meaning cannot be found on a superficial level.

Although the speaker contemplates the mule throughout most of the poem, he occasionally breaks into the poetic discourse to address the animal directly. This procedure calls attention to the speaker's presence and directs the reader's interest to the relationship between the poetic voice and the mule. The speaker's repeated meditation on the mule's destiny leads the reader to suspect that the poetic voice actively identifies with the animal. This connection is most striking in the passage about the mule's relation to creativity.

> El no puede, no crea ni persigue,
> ni brincan sus ojos
> ni sus ojos buscan el secuestrado asilo
> al borde preñado de la tierra.
> No crea, eso es tal vez decir:
> ¿No siente, no ama ni pregunta? (53; A4)

Creativity is one of the poem's major preoccupations, and it is linked frequently to the issue of sterility. The above quotation is followed by lines that underscore the mule's loyalty to and love for the source of his origin. This fidelity has been created not by promises of redemption or heaven, but by thankfulness for the gift of life.[7]

> Su amor a los cuatro signos
> del desfiladero, a las sucesivas coronas
> en que asciende vidrioso, cegato,
> como un oscuro cuerpo hinchado
> por el agua de los orígenes,
> no la de la redención y los perfumes.
> Paso es el paso del mulo en el abismo. (53; A5)

The mule's response to the gift of life is his steady gait, each step moving him on his journey through the abyss. His persis-

---

7. These sentiments recall a classic poem from the colonial period: Miguel de Guevara's "No me mueves, mi Dios."

tence begins to overcome sterility. However, the speaker suggests that some observers confuse the animal's steady march with sterility:

> Ese seguro paso del mulo en el abismo
> suele confundirse con los pintados guantes de lo estéril.
> Suele confundirse con los comienzos
> de la oscura cabeza negadora.
> Por ti suele confundirse, descastado vidrioso. (55; A6)

The speaker again addresses the mule directly, and the association of sterility and creativity closes in the above quotation with a metaphor that likens the mule to a "descastado vidrioso." The reference to glass ("vidrioso") recalls the glassiness of the mule's eyes in the first lines of the poem, but the word *descastado* introduces a new note, which is soon repeated. One of the meanings of *descastar* is "to separate or stand apart." Within the context of its appearance, *descastado* most clearly resembles the word *outcast* in English. But it can also mean "acabar con una casta de animales, por lo común dañinos"[8] (to put an end to a usually harmful type of animal). This implies that the mule is an object of hostility and that he is mistakenly regarded as a sterile outcast. At the end of the poem, however, the mule engenders trees—an indication that his nonproductive condition has been overcome.

> Paso es el paso, cajas de agua, fajado por Dios
> el poderoso mulo duerme temblando.
> Con sus ojos sentados y acuosos,
> al fin el mulo árboles encaja en todo abismo. (57; A7)

Eduardo Forastieri Braschi, in a concise and insightful article, has described "Rapsodia para el mulo" as a manifestation of a poetical system based on theodicy and ontology.[9] That is, he sees the work as a defense of God's goodness in view of the evil in the world and as a study of the nature and relations of being. The extent to which "Rapsodia" is a defense of God's goodness may be debatable. But there is in the poem an acceptance of the harshness of life and of God's plan. There is

---

8. *Diccionario de la lengua española de la Real Academia* (Madrid: Espasa Calpe, 1970), s.v. "descastar."
9. Forastieri Braschi, "Nota al 'aspa volteando incesante oscuro,'" 141.

undoubtedly a religious code operating in the work—a code that can be seen in the frequent mentions of God, the references to the cross and nails, and the recurrent image of "the four signs (the four hooves of Christ's stigmata)."[10] The mule's relationship to this religious code is one of the most expansive elements in the poem, and the reader can identify with the speaker's questions about the meaning of suffering in existence.

Although a mule, a humble animal is seemingly unworthy of the exalted role it has in this work, this paradox is central to the meaning of the poem. Since a mule is a hybrid of a horse and an ass, it can be considered a synthesis of the symbolism traditionally associated with these origins. One need only recall the donkey's role in the birth and life of Christ to recognize its association with humility and service in a divine mission. The symbolism of the horse is more complex, but within the context of the work, it operates as the opposite of an ass, that is, as a mystical and superior force that contrasts with the mundane and humble role of its counterpart. The reader is invited to view the imagery of the mule simultaneously on literal and figurative levels. On the one hand, the mule is a beast of burden noted for its physical endurance; on the other, it suggests persistence and effort on a more imaginative and creative plane. As a metaphor, the mule points toward the past, its origins, as well as toward the future goal of its mission. Lezama Lima has indicated that the mule's diligent journey through space is like the creative imagination's struggles against time. "La resistencia del mulo siembra en el abismo, como la duración poética siembra resurgiendo en lo estelar. Uno, resiste en el cuerpo, otro, resiste en el tiempo, y a ambos se les ve su aleta buscando el complemento desconocido, conocido, desconocido"[11] (A8). This dialectical movement be-

10. Rothrock Lutz, "Poetry of Lezama Lima," 118. Religious code is used here in the sense that Roland Barthes refers to a cultural code. For an interesting modification of Barthes's codes, which are presented in his book *S/Z*, see Andrew Debicki, "Códigos expresivos en el *Romancero gitano*," *Texto Crítico* 5, no. 14 (July–September 1979): 143–54. For an application of Barthes's codes to a Cuban novel, see John S. Brushwood, "Structuration of the Narrative Text: Ramón Meza's *Mi tío el empleado*," chap. 6 in his *Genteel Barbarism*, 107–38.

11. Lezama Lima, *Las eras imaginarias*, 189–90.

tween the known and the unknown is paralleled by the mule's literal and figurative roles, as the ordinary is transformed into the divine in a creative as well as a religious sense. The mundane mule becomes a synthesis of the material and the spiritual, or a manifestation of the poetic voice's desire to transform the ordinary into an embodiment of the infinite.

"Rapsodia para el mulo" can also be regarded as a meditation on the role of the individual in a number of ethical and social contexts, and as a consideration of the source of personal worth. The speaker's identification with the mule, the acceptance of the sacrificial challenges of life and death, and the affirmation of creativity in the face of sterility, form parallels between the mule and the poetic voice. Forastieri Braschi suggests indirectly that the mule is a substitution for the poet Lezama Lima.[12] This observation is a brilliant insight, for Lezama Lima, who through personal choice never engendered any offspring, at times must have felt like a marginal member of society because of his childless state and his dedication to poetry. In the poem the mule is rewarded—he goes to heaven.

"Rapsodia" is an affirmation of spiritual origins and a plea for legitimacy and acceptance, concerns that found their maximum expression in *Paradiso*. Lezama Lima's incorporation of family history and an autobiographical mode into *Paradiso* will be studied in Chapter 5, but it should be mentioned at this point that the search for origins and the quest for legitimacy mark much of his work. This search suggests the incorporation of the self into social units and traditions that nurture and justify the existence of the individual.

"Rapsodia para el mulo" contains an undercurrent of anguish produced by the harshness of existence, but this minor motif is subordinated to the refuge offered by faith. In "Los fragmentos de la noche," however, the speaker's inability to fathom a life plan predominates.

12. Forastieri Braschi, "Nota al 'aspa volteando incesante oscuro.'" A more recent statement about the poem made by Eloísa Lezama Lima makes the same connection: "Yo lo he asociado a nuestro diálogo donde me insistía, refiriéndose a su terca vocación: 'Soy un mulo con orejas que va a su destino.' . . . *Vida, pasión y creación de José Lezama Lima: fechas claves para una cronología*" (Eloísa Lezama Lima, "Bibliografía," 27).

"Los fragmentos de la noche" is the third of three poems placed together under the title "Doble noche" (heavy night).[13] The first two compositions are very brief and untitled except for the numerical designations "I" and "II," and they operate as motif setters for "Los fragmentos de la noche." The first poem suggests the beauty as well as the dangers of the night— "la noche nos agarra un pie, / nos clava en un árbol" (night grasps a foot, / nails us to a tree)—and focuses on its mysterious and enigmatic qualities. In the second poem, the speaker relates personal identity to the body and communicates the desire to illuminate the enigmas the night represents with the light of understanding. Both poems close with references to a cat, an animal noted for its nocturnal wanderings and, when it is black, for its linkage to darkness and death. In the first poem, the cat claws a hole in the earth—"ha fabricado un agujero húmedo" (it has made a humid hole)—and both works close with references to the cat hiding the night—I: "Hace trampa / y esconde de nuevo a la noche" (It cheats / and again hides the night); II: "El gato absorto y lentísimo / comenzó de nuevo a esconder la noche" (The engrossed cat very slowly / begins again to hide the night). The hole the cat makes is associated with the negative qualities of the night and with a terrible and repugnant mystery that creates anxiety in the speaker. This enigma is as intimately known as the body and is as eerie and uncanny as darkness. The mystery is present but inaccessible, absent but known. The cat's act of burying the night as it would its own wastes indicates that the threatening mystery the night symbolizes is suppressed.

In "Los fragmentos de la noche" the speaker wages an active struggle against the unknown the night represents and attempts to capture and unite the night's fragments the way one would put together a physical entity.

> Cómo aislar los fragmentos de la noche
> para apretar algo con las manos,
> como la liebre penetra en su oscuridad
> separando dos estrellas

13. Lezama Lima, "Doble noche," in his *Fragmentos a su imán*. The following quotes have been taken from the 1978 Ediciones Era edition.

apoyadas en el brillo de la yerba húmeda.
La noche respira en una intocable humedad,
no en el centro de la esfera que vuela,
y todo lo va uniendo, esquinas o fragmentos,
hasta formar el irrompible tejido de la noche,
sutil y completo como los dedos unidos
que apenas dejan pasar el agua,
como un cestillo mágico
que nada vacío dentro del río. (78–79; A9)

The reference to moist grass recalls the humid hole of the first poem, and the expression is followed by a string of water-based metonymical associations that are strategically placed throughout the text. At one point in the poem, water becomes a substitution for night, and the speaker's struggle to unravel the riddle of existence is compared to the untying of an anchored barge.

Yo quería rescatar los fragmentos de la noche
y formaba una sustancia universal,
comencé entonces a sumergir
los dedos y los ojos en la noche,
le soltaba todas las amarras a la barcaza.
Era un combate sin término,
entre lo que yo le quería quitar a la noche
y lo que la noche me regalaba. (79; A10)

The struggle is endless and the speaker feels defeated. The deep waters of the sea, like the night, represent the mysteries of death, a reality the speaker would prefer to avoid.

The hare that is introduced in the third sentence of the poem appears in the central section and in the final lines of the work. Only sleep can prevent the hare from tormenting the speaker, yet as the poem ends, the hare leaves scars on his face.

Como en un incendio,
yo quería sacar los recuerdos de la noche,
el tintineo hacia dentro del golpe mate,
como cuando con la palma de la mano
golpeamos la masa de pan.
El sueñno volvió a detener a la liebre
que arañba mis brazos
con palillos de aguarrás.
Riéndose, repartía por mi rostro grandes cicatrices. (80; A11)

The act of falling asleep suggests a drifting off into death, and here the hare is clearly a substitution for an aspect of the speaker: his consciousness, which attempts to understand death; or perhaps his imagination, which will only cease when he dies. In the first lines of the poem, the attempt to unite the fragments of the night is likened to the hare's efforts to penetrate the darkness that separates two stars. Just as the night is a period of blackness between the light of two days, death is a stage between existence on earth and the promised resurrection. But the speaker's attempts to understand this mystery of faith are defeated, and he is left with the tormented agitation of his own mind. Since the hare represents an aspect of the speaker's being, it can be surmised that the cat in the first two poems is also a substitution; it represents the speaker's fear. Just as the cat buries its own excrement in the sand, the speaker attempts to suppress the repugnant reality that death represents. But he recognizes that his identity is linked to the existence of his body, and his consciousness, represented by the hare that scratches his face, does not permit him to avoid this terrible specter. The speaker's linkage to material reality is intensified by the physicality of the poem, that is, by its many references to the concrete world and by its presentation of the night as a material entity. The poetic voice is frustrated by its inability to grasp death's meaning, and this suggests a reluctance to accept the demise of the body. The fear of the death of the body is also subtly suggested by a sexual code that is embedded in the poem. This code communicates the poetic voice's reluctance to surrender its identity to the forces that originally gave life.

In this work, the speaker fails to find any comforting coherence in the world, and he is left only with dark forbodings. The use of animals as substitutions for aspects of the poetic voice recalls the role of the mule in "Rapsodia para el mulo," but there is less faith and more despair in the three sections of "Doble noche."

Fragmentos a su imán contains Lezama Lima's most intimate and direct poetry, while exhibiting an autobiographical mode in many of its works. His quest for unity and harmony—a persistent search that underlies most of his publications—also marks this volume. In many poems the speaker finds glimpses of wholeness in the daily routine of life, but these brief encounters with completeness are counterbalanced by a series of poems in which the speaker struggles unsuccessfully against incomprehension and chaos. Works such as "Doble noche" suggest that the confusion and torment of the world cannot be overcome and contrast with earlier works such as "Rapsodia para el mulo."

In the last poem of *Fragmentos a su imán,* "Pabellón del vacío," which is dated 1 April 1976 and is believed to be the last poetic work Lezama Lima wrote, the speaker seeks refuge in a niche in a wall, or a "tokonoma," which is a Japanese alcove used for the display of various art forms. This withdrawal from the world and merging with the void offers a degree of comfort. "Me voy reduciendo, / soy un punto que desaparece y vuelve / y quepo entero en el *tokonoma*" (A12). But the poem closes with a question and an affirmation that communicate the speaker's desire to separate the spirit and the flesh. "¿La aridez en el vacío / es el primer y último camino? / Me duermo, en el tokonoma / evaporo el otro que sigue caminando" (A13). The duality of body and idea seems to be overcome, but there are doubts about whether the "other" entirely disappears and whether the self-referentiality of the "I" is completely overcome. This is one of the central dilemmas in Lezama Lima's works—one that will be examined in Chapter 5.

"Pabellón del vacío" considers the dichotomies of self and other, life and death, and here and there, but these binary oppositions cannot be resolved and they fail to disappear completely. His sister probably had compositions such as this one in mind when she suggested that the reading of *Fragmentos a su imán* exposed the reader to some of the vulnerabilities of Lezama Lima's last thoughts.[14] Although the speaker expresses the desire to merge with the void in "Pabellón del vacío," there is also a reluctance to give up the awareness of being a singular entity located in a specific point in space and a precise moment in time.

Fragmentos a su imán and *Oppiano Licario,* which both

14. Eloísa Lezama Lima, "*Fragmentos a su imán:* últimos poemas de José Lezama Lima," 21.

appeared after Lezama Lima's death in 1976, are more concise and less hermetic than his previous works, an indication of his movement toward understanding and clarity of expression. Although *Paradiso* is a formidable and complex work, it is generally conceded that it is easier to comprehend than his poetry, a conviction that Lezama Lima has reinforced: "Para llegar a mi novela, hubo necesidad de escribir mis ensayos y de escribir mis poemas. Yo dije varias veces que cuando me sentía claro escribía prosa y cuando me sentía oscuro escribía poesía. Es decir, mi trabajo oscuro es la poesía y mi trabajo de evidencia, buscando lo central, lo más meridiano que podía configurar en mis ensayos, tiene como consecuencia la perspectiva de *Paradiso*"[15] (A14). However, in the last two works this relationship is inverted, and the poetry of *Fragmentos* is easier to understand than the prose of *Oppiano Licario*. This inversion is most likely due to Lezama Lima's interest in synthesizing the two genres and to the incorporation of some features of his fiction into his poetry. The transposition of difficulty is also related to his awareness of the limits of human knowledge and the failure of all systems, including that of his own poetics, to completely master or understand the world. However, like Don Quijote, who failed to rid the world of evil, and like the Modernist poets, who never completely succeeded in their attempts to capture beauty, Lezama Lima's struggles to achieve the impossible resulted in the creation of monumental works. One of the manifestations of his interest in achieving unity was the effort to integrate fiction and poetry, and this enterprise frequently resulted in the creation of what can be termed metonymical poetry and metaphorical prose. However, these terms should not be regarded as mutually exclusive, for an intimate relation frequently exists between metaphor and metonymy in Lezama Lima's works. We will consider this connection in the following chapter, particularly as it is manifested in his most ambitious search for unity—*Paradiso*.

15. "Interrogando a Lezama Lima," in *Recopilación de textos sobre José Lezama Lima*, ed. Pedro Simón Martínez, 25.

2

Metaphor and Metonymy in *Paradiso*

When Lezama Lima was asked in an interview if he considered *Paradiso* a "novela-poema," he answered: "Indudablemente que es una novela-poema en el sentido en que se aparta del concepto habitual de lo que es una novela. *Paradiso* está basado en la metáfora, en la imagen; está basado en la negación del tiempo, negación de los accidentes y en ese sentido sus recursos de expresión son casi esencialmente poéticos"[1] (A15). Lezama Lima's statement contains a number of important points. To him *Paradiso* is a denial of randomness and time and is grounded in metaphorical expression. This association of metaphor with both timelessness and the negation of disorder points to an inherent contradiction within his conception of the novel. If there are no accidental occurrences, one must assume that all events have an explanation and are ruled by a system or a process of cause and effect. Events are therefore time-bound. However, if metaphors constitute a denial of time, they must incorporate elements that are time-free. Lezama Lima's declarations indicate he was aware that he was creating a synthesis of poetry and fiction, which suggests that he had to struggle with the issue of combining story and metaphor, that is, with the categorization of time-bound and time-free elements. In consideration of this problem, this chapter focuses on the manner in which metaphor and metonymy operate in *Paradiso* and considers the overall importance of these figures in his works.

In a study on the semantics of metaphor, Umberto Eco suggests that metaphor can be based on a network of metonymic chains or connections.[2] If one considers metaphor to be a

1. "Interrogando a Lezama Lima," in *Recopilación de textos sobre José Lezama Lima,* ed. Pedro Simón Martínez, 27.
2. Eco, "The Semantics of Metaphor," chap. 2 in his *The Role of the Reader,* 67–89. For a concise and comprehensive survey of the evolution of metaphor

substitution based on analogy and metonymy, a substitution based on association, then the type of relationship that leads to a metaphoric or metonymic connection becomes crucial. If the relationship is based on similarity, it is metaphoric; if it is based on contiguity, it is metonymic. In his analysis of metonymic functions, Eco distinguishes between factual and semiotic associations. He points out, for example, that the substitution of *crown* for *king* is based on the fact that a king wears a crown, and that the term *white-collar worker* has the same type of origin. However, it is no longer necessary that an employee wear a white collar to be designated by that term. This is an indication that the relationship is no longer factual but is instead semiotic.

It is Eco's contention that metaphor rests on metonymy and that metaphor exists because it short-circuits a series of associations contained in a metonymic network. "A metaphor can be invented because language, in its process of unlimited semiosis, constitutes a multidimensional network of metonymies, each of which is explained by a cultural convention rather than an original resemblance."[3] As relationships extend and become further removed from the original factual basis, the possibility that they will be designated as metaphors rather than metonymies increases. The term *white-collar worker*, for example, was originally a substitution based on association—the wearing of a white shirt—but it has become a substitution based on analogy, that is, a correspondence of function that designates a certain class of workers, no matter what type of clothing they wear.

One of the functions of imaginative language is to uncover connections that have never been recognized—a process that leads to the creation of ambiguous messages, which create tension. Eco suggests that metaphor relies "upon possible contradictions of the code."[4] As language increases the range of possible correspondences, a word's meaning may be changed or modified. As a result, a signifier may indicate a

---

and metonymy in several fields, see Floyd Merrell, "Metaphor and Metonymy." This article contains extensive bibliographical information.

3. Eco, *Role of the Reader*, 78.
4. Ibid., 87.

signified that "is not its own."[5] As connections along a metonymic chain extend, the possibility of contradiction increases. Eco concludes that "in order for the Global Semantic System to be able to produce creative utterances, *it is necessary* that it be self-contradictory and that no *Form* of content exist, only *forms* of content."[6] Eco's contention that contradiction is inherent in the process that generates metonymic and metaphoric relationships is of fundamental importance.

Roman Jakobson has pointed out that imaginative language makes use of both metaphoric and metonymic modes and that "in poetry where similarity is superinduced upon contiguity, any metonymy is slightly metaphorical and any metaphor has a metonymical tint."[7] He has also stated, "The principal of similarity underlies poetry. . . . Prose on the contrary, is forwarded essentially by contiguity. Thus, for poetry, metaphor, and for prose, metonymy, is the line of least resistance."[8] Since Jakobson indicates that metonymy tends to be the prominent feature of prose and metaphor the major element of poetry, his comments on these modes can be helpful in any attempt to describe the unusual features of *Paradiso*. His observations also shed light on Lezama Lima's endeavors to merge poetry and prose fiction, and his contention that the poetic function of language projects metaphor into the realm of metonymy is particularly applicable to Lezama Lima's works.[9]

5. Ibid.
6. Ibid., 88.
7. Jakobson, "Closing Statement," 370.
8. Roman Jakobson and Morris Halle, *Fundamentals of Language*, 81–82.
9. Jakobson believes that metaphoric and metonymic modes are essentially competitive: "A competition between both devices, metonymic and metaphoric, is manifest in any symbolic process, either interpersonal or social. Thus in an inquiry into the structure of dreams, the decisive question is whether the symbols and the temporal sequences used are based on contiguity (Freud's metonymic 'displacement' and synecdochic 'condensation') or on similarity (Freud's 'identification and symbolism'). The principles underlying magic rites have been resolved by Frazer into two types: charms based on the law of similarity and those founded on association by contiguity" (ibid., 80–81). Jakobson's references to the works of Sigmund Freud and James Frazer are highly suggestive, for although he is dealing with the basic functions of language, his comments imply that metaphoric and metonymic modes reflect fundamental ways of thinking. An interesting application and modification of Jakobson's concepts is available in David Lodge, *The Modes of Modern Writing* (Ithaca, N.Y.: Cornell University Press, 1977). See particularly pp. 73–81 and 113–24.

One of the startling results of metonymic and metaphoric processes is that they can disclose similarities where none seem to exist and reveal relationships that are not readily apparent. In many respects, Lezama Lima's art represents an attempt to uncover and exalt the multitude of hidden relationships that contribute to the mystery of existence. Indeed, the essence of his art seems to be the search for epiphanic, combinatory possibilities.

In chapter 5 of *Paradiso*, a blackboard is referred to as a "black beach." "Y desde la misma distancia del sillar babilónico de Aredo lanzó el compás sobre la playa negra"[10] (A16). Although the connection may not be immediately apparent, the adjective *black* establishes an association that is based on reality in the physical world, for not only is its use in the term *blackboard* appropriate, but it is also aptly used in the construction *black beach*—black beaches, consisting of volcanic sand, do exist. Yet the term *playa negra* (black beach) is an intriguing term to use in referring to a blackboard, and it immediately strikes the reader as an expansive element. At first glance the color black seems to be the only similarity between *pizarrón* (blackboard) and *playa negra*. But since white is the color usually associated with beaches, the use of the color black is particularly ingenious: black displaces white, causing the reader to be aware of the two colors simultaneously. As a result, the opposition black/white conveys a sense of contending or opposing forces, which intensifies the sense of opposition already conveyed by the word *beach*, since it signifies an area where the land and ocean meet. And just as a beach forms a barrier where the force of the sea meets the land, in *Paradiso* the blackboard marks a limit that receives the violence of a character's anger.

The individual who throws the compass is Fibo, one of Aredo's classmates, and his action is born of anger and frustration. The description of Aredo's desk as "Babylonian" is the second such description of the desk. The first reference, which appears fourteen pages earlier in chapter 4, has little meaning

10. Lezama Lima, *Paradiso* (Mexico City: Ediciones Era, 1968), 103. Subsequent quotations are from this edition and are noted in the text.

because it has no context, but the second use of the description has significance because of events that have occurred in the interim—events that have established a series of associations.

The metonymic chain that gives context to the second reference to Aredo's desk is established in a scenario that involves another classmate, Alberto Olaya. Alberto's antics during an English class attract the wrath of the headmaster, who punishes Alberto by sending him to take a shower—a chastisement that strikes terror in the hearts of the other students. The shower stalls are described as if they were part of a dungeon, and the network of pipes leading to the shower and to the showerhead is depicted in mythological terms. "En el cruzamiento, emparejados, pero irreconciliables, de los tubos de plomo, en la tronada de la ducha, el ave de Angra Mainyu, que despierta como la muerte" (100; A17).

Angra Mainyu, a principle figure from Persian mythology, was the antagonist of "the omniscient Lord, Ahura Mazda. . . . These two personages marked the two poles of existence. . . . They could be defined by their antagonism: the god as anti-demon, the demon as anti-god. The real world was the result of their hand to hand struggle. All was conflict between these two principles."[11] Angra Mainyu, a subversive force, continually attempted to counteract the creations of Ahura Mazda. Angra Mainyu produced death to counteract life, darkness to put out light, falsehood to confuse truth, doubt to undermine faith, and cold to retard the growth of living things. Lezama Lima makes several allusions to these functions.

Fibo's throwing of the compass occurs after Aredo returns from a trip to the shower room, where he has observed Alberto, and tells Fibo what he has seen. Upon entering the shower, Aredo discovers that Alberto had fallen asleep after having masturbated: "Olaya estaba desnudamente dormido, la ropa hinchada por el descuido, náufrago que ha puesto su ropa al fuego. Apoyada la espalda en la pared donde crecía el esternón de plomo de la ducha. Detenida entre el índice y el anillo de la mano derecha, la flor del sexo pendía en el hastío final de la desnudez, cuando el sueño comienza a inclinarnos en la

---

11. Felix Guirand, ed., *New Larousse Encyclopedia of Mythology*, 315–16.

primera victoria de Angra Mainyu, que despierta como la muerte" (101; A18).

The association of dreaming with Angra Mainyu and death denotes a partial victory of negative forces, for Alberto's falling asleep is paralleled by the deity's awakening. In the cold and damp shower stall, Alberto's semen has swirled into a drain, and possible life has succumbed to cold. But in a contradictory process that is typical of Lezama Lima's works, Alberto's dream world offers other choices. In the drain Alberto sees Aredo and another classmate, José Eugenio Cemí, and each of these figures is associated with either negative or positive forces. There are sacrificial and undesirable overtones in the description of Aredo's figure. His left leg is naked and a wild boar with "a flaccid head" is carried in.[12] The flaccidity, or softness, of the boar's head seems to refer to the diabolical urges that Aredo's soft body provokes in Fibo, and there are sexual connotations in these associations. José Eugenio's figure, on the other hand, counteracts these negative forces, for he is seen pouring water from a pitcher to a glass, an action that gives form to and contains the water. This provides a contrast to the cascade of water from the shower, which is associated with Angra Mainyu, and to Alberto's spilling of his seed. These associations point toward positive and negative expressions of sexuality—Fibo and Aredo suggest a perversion of sexual instincts, while José Eugenio represents the control of these forces.

A curious and startling technical device is used when Alberto leaves the shower. At one point the reader is confused as to whether it is Alberto or José Eugenio who is abandoning the shower. This implied synthesis is clearly intentional. Alberto flees the school and that evening experiences his first amorous encounter with a young girl. Here his sensuality finds a more fecund expression than it had in the sterile environment of the shower room. In light of this experience, the intentional confu-

12. Juan Eduardo Cirlot points out that the left side can be associated "with the past, the sinister, the repressed, involution, the abnormal and the illegitimate; the right side with the future, the felicitous, openness, evolution, the normal and legitimate" (Cirlot, *A Dictionary of Symbols*, 287).

sion about the character's identity at the end of the shower scene suggests associations that point toward the future, for Alberto becomes the point of contact between José Eugenio and his future wife.

A reference in the above scene to Alberto as a castaway is a substitution that rests on a metonymic network that extends throughout this section of the text. There are a number of replacements that are based on associations related to the sea. When Alberto and José Eugenio go to school on the first day of classes, a number of complex references to the ocean appears in the text. The imagery in this passage thickens as it presents a highly defamiliarized scene.[13]

> Fue Alberto el primero que representó la sospesa al penetrar en el aula, fue el primero que sorprendió y se bebió el espacio, rasgado levemente por las nuevas respiraciones que venían a agujerearlo, a establecer, durante una estación, sus madreporarios para aquellas colonias dermatitas de los recuerdos entrecruzados y de los flagelos que se descargaban, a través de una niebla que al ser pinchada devolvía urdicantes, como expresión de los complementos protoplasmáticos.
>
> Al entrar en el aula José Eugenio, la figura que menos aclaró en sus primeros recorridos por el espejeante y maravilloso monstruo que se tendía a su alcance, fue la del maestro. Veía entre la niebla y el follaje, monstruo de tridentes, poliedros que se entreabrían desenrollando flagelos nerviosos, como un caballito de mar posado en la caparazón de un tortugón tricentenario. Y en frente otro monstruo, irreconciliable con el primero, que lo sorprendía por su fija extensión y el matinal tegumento de su piel. Comenzaba a penetrar en el monstruo de la extensión, cuando el pequeño director desde su concha, comenzó a descifrarse, como si fuese extrayendo sus coloreados mamelucos ante la maliciosa intención de los proyectores para sus perversiones y sus monosílabos. (87; A19)

In this scene, which evokes as much as it describes, three figures are perceived by José Eugenio: ''el maestro,'' ''el

13. Victor Shklovsky has defined *defamiliarization* as follows: ''The purpose of art is to impart the sensation of things as they are perceived and not as they are known. The technique of art is to make objects 'unfamiliar,' to make forms difficult, to increase the difficulty and length of perception because the process of perception is an aesthetic end in itself and must be prolonged'' (Shklovsky, ''Art as Technique,'' in *Russian Formalist Criticism*, ed. and trans. Lee T. Lemon and Marion J. Reis, 12).

epejeante y maravilloso monstruo,'' and ''el monstruo de la extensión'' (A20). In the pages that follow this passage, a transformation of the second figure occurs: ''el espejeante y maravilloso monstruo'' in subsequent references is ''la superficie plateada del ballenato,'' (88) and ''el ballenato, el monstruo de piel plateada'' (89). ''Monstruo'' is replaced by ''ballenato,'' and then the two terms appear together. ''Espejeante'' becomes ''superficie plateada'' and ''piel plateada.'' The two lines of associations then merge in ''la blanda corpulencia de Enrique Aredo, la lechosa provocación de su piel'' (90).

The other enigmatic figure in the trio witnessed by José Eugenio is first referred to as ''the other monster'' and then as ''the monster of erection.'' These images refer to Fibo, whose satanic passion is to prick unwary classmates with a mechanical pen. Although there are a number of negative references to Fibo's pen, it also becomes associated with the energy that is able to counteract the monster's indifference. A basic opposition is therefore established between dynamic and static forces. The ritual of Fibo's lancing of Aredo is first foreshadowed in the text by the statement: ''Pero muy pronto la superficie plateada del ballenato iba a ser raspada por una oruga elástica'' (88; A21). This sentence appears in the text just as the classroom is beginning to surrender to boredom; the term ''elastic caterpillar'' suggests the diabolical energy that is about to be unleashed.

The passage describing Alberto and José Eugenio's entrance into the classroom contains numerous direct references to the sea and the life within it (coral reefs, fog, tridents, sea horses, and the shell of a turtle) as well as indirect references—to microscopic sea life and algae (flagella and polyhedrons). Given the inherent multidimensional nature of such a complex network in addition to Lezama Lima's ability to suggest multiple meanings, a further consideration of the implications of some of these figures is in order. Tridents and sea horses are usually associated with Neptune, who ''symbolizes the negative aspect of the spirit. He is king of the deeps of the subconscious and of the turbulent waters of life; it is he who unleashes storms—representing the passions of the soul—particularly in his extreme role as the destroyer." The trident is often seen as "an emblem of the threefold sin arising from the corruption of the three 'vital impluses' of the spirit (conservation, reproduction and evolution)"; it "is also an attribute of Satan."[14] The trident is also associated with the Hindu deity Siva, who has a destructive role; but according to one source, this deity is "everywhere worshipped as the principle of generation under the symbol of the lingarn (phallus)."[15] No matter which references are consulted, the two figures are associated with both generative and destructive forces and, ultimately, with the paradoxical origins of good and evil.

Lezama Lima moves from the specific to the archetypal in passages such as this one and uses characteristics or elements attributed to one object in order to describe another, independent entity. His movement between mythical and empirical realms allows him to combine time-bound and time-free elements. While specific associations are open to interpretation, the quoted passage as a whole suggests excitement and danger. The new and strange environment of school on the first day elicits unknown sensations that are much like those that might accompany immersion into the sea. Alberto and José Eugenio are in an unfamiliar world of unsuspected correspondences and complex interconnections, a place that is at once stimulating and threatening.

The metonymic chain of sea-related associations is the basis for many metaphoric substitutions. Some examples, including a few that have already been mentioned, are "ballenato" (88; A22) for student, "los arenales más blandos del cuerpo" (89) for buttocks, "el ballenato, el monstruo de piel plateada" (89) for a student who is the object of Fibo's aggressive stabs, "el júbilo de los cazones cuando rodean un salmón homérico" (92) for student athletes swarming around a ball, "tinta de calamar" (96) for inkwell, "como el vacío chupado por el calamar para elaborar su tinta excepcionalmente albina" (100) for soapsuds going down a shower drain, and "playa negra" (103) for blackboard. A further extension of this chain exists in the

14. Cirlot, *Dictionary of Symbols*, 217.
15. Guirand, *Encyclopedia of Mythology*, 374.

sentence preceding the appearance of "black beach." The compass that is hurled against the blackboard is described as being the size of a "blind crab." After sinking into the blackboard, it makes a sound like that of a crab chewing on a palm leaf.

The compass can be seen as a synthesis of Fibo and Aredo. Although it is Aredo's compass, Fibo is the one who, with Aredo's cooperation, throws it at the blackboard, in which it becomes embedded. In addition, the compass has been associated throughout the chapter with Aredo, and the pencil, an infernal instrument of penetration—which is, in this instance, attached to the hurled compass—with Fibo. This recalls the earlier association of "the monster of erection" with Fibo and his pencil and of the trident (like the compass, an object with multiple points) with Aredo. Fibo and his classroom antics are often referred to in negative terms, as manifestations of the darker side of existence. Yet some of his frustration has sexual connotations. When he hurls the compass against the wall, it is possible that the blackboard represents feminine sexuality to him. His act suggests his as-yet-unfulfilled sexuality and also prefigures Alberto's imminent sexual fulfillment on his first night away from home with a girl.

The paragraph in which Fibo is fully described opens with the statement: "En aquel primer día de clase iba José Eugenio a inaugurar el primer día de contemplación de maldad en su pura gratuidad; la primera demostración que veía, más allá de la dificultad conciliar *quod erat demonstrandum*, de la incontrovertible existencia del pecado original en cada criatura" (88; A23). This mention of the belief that original sin is a presence that marks all beings explains in part Lezama Lima's proclivity for using paradoxical imagery. Sometimes his characters are physically marked in a way that suggests an innate defect. In the first scene of the novel, for example, the infant José Cemí, the son of José Eugenio Cemí, suffers an attack of asthma, and his body is covered with angry welts that steadily increase in size. The servants engage in a spiritual exercise in an attempt to exorcize the evil that possesses him, and the reader is left to ponder whether José's recovery is related to the strange ritual. Another example of such a physical marking is the dark rings under Fibo's eyes—an indication of his role in the novel. The technique of using negative marks as manifestations of innate defects reflects Lezama Lima's complex view of reality.

Fibo and Aredo's attempts to direct their emotions are conveyed by the throwing of the compass. After it hits the wall, the side with the pencil swings around, forming semi-circles in a subtle manifestation of the most pervasive image in *Paradiso*, the circle. In this case, the compass represents an elemental attempt to give form to emotion and to gain control over forces that are not understood. The headmaster of the school, Cuevarolliot, extracts the compass from the wall as if it were a tooth being torn from flesh and bone and then goes to find Alberto in the shower. The prisoner has escaped his damp prison, leaving behind only cigarette butts as an indication of his former presence. The headmaster vents his rage by pounding one leg of the compass against a door and then stomping on the cigarette butts and their ashes. The actions of the pompous schoolmaster parallel those of Fibo, for both use the compass to vent their rage. However, they proceed from different ends of a spectrum formed by the extremes of dynamic chaos and rigid order. Fibo threatens to upset the tranquility of the classroom with his frenetic jabs, while the headmaster's inept and tyrannical use of authority has a stifling effect. Fibo is a sign of chaotic or misguided forces, Cuevarolliot, an embodiment of repressive power. In each case physical force is directed against an object that contains the raging energy: a wall and a floor.

The scene in which Cuevarolliot enters the shower contains a number of mythological associations, and many of these are based on fire and water. A series of associations progresses from cigarettes to ashes to fire, and references to water are present in the sound of the shower and the mention of the Greek river god Inachus.

> Picó ferozmente con el compás en la puerta de la mazmorra, pero se encontró conque dentro de la caja, el desencordelado había dejado tan sólo las huellas de los cigarrillos vencidos. Intentó destruir la esencial simetría con sus zapatos voraces, fulmíneo pisapapel en zigzagueante túmulo sobre las cenizas.

> Eran los recuerdos que quedaban de la sombriamente movili-
> zada hija de Inaco, la enloquecida Io, apresada entre el recuerdo
> de la música de las duchas y los cigarrillos pisoteados por la furia
> de Cuevarolliot, sobras de un Argos que no habían podido
> impedir la fuga. Pero el pequeño claveteado, que conversaba con
> el resentido cariño de la hija de Inaco, se había apoderado del
> primer día en que rodaría su fuego rescatado. (103; A24)

The web of associations, involving numerous elements and
mythological figures, leads to an indirect reference to Zeus and
actual mention of Io, one of his consorts. The reference to
rescued fire suggests Prometheus, who stole fire from Zeus
and whose relationship to him was one of rebellion. The rebel
in this scene from *Paradiso* is Alberto, who has successfully
defied Cuevarolliot and escaped his punishment. Several elements in this episode are reminiscent of the encounter between Prometheus and Io, which occurs in a major scene in
Aeschylus's *Prometheus Bound.* Io, maddened by the gadfly, a
destructive insect sent by Juno, escapes. In a subversion of the
myth's chronology, Alberto partially escapes his punishment
by smoking a cigarette. The sign of his victory is a triumphant
firefly, a metaphor for a cigarette that is based on the metonymic chain of mythological relationships that link Zeus and fire.
"Gozosa luciérnaga bañándose en la música de la oscuridad
incorporada, al llegar Alberto Olaya a la esquina del colegio,
encendió un cigarro clarineante" (103; A25). Inachus intensifies the basic opposition of fire and water and leads back to the
realm of the shower and Angra Mainyu, José Eugenio, Fibo,
Aredo, Neptune, and Siva. This summary of this metonymic
chain leaves out many links, but the essential outline is present
in the figures cited. The network of associations extends
throughout the rest of the chapter and radiates in all directions
throughout the novel.

Alberto's struggles with adversity are not over; he is subjected to other trials. He rejects the sexual advances of an old
man, whose attempts are associated with Siva, and rescues a
young girl from the undesirable attentions of the same man.
Significantly, to soothe her anger and fear, he gives her a
mechanical pencil with four colors of lead. He is unlike Fibo,
who uses his mechanical pencil as an instrument of torment,

and his gift leads to his seduction of the girl and his first night away from home. The girl's sensuality and desirability are captured in her green eyes. The overwhelming passion they feel as they enter a hotel room is conveyed by the association of a crippled housemaid's leg with a mermaid's tail. The housemaid sings as they enter the room, but when they leave they decide that the negative forces she represents will be controlled. "La sirena del relator, que acudió sonando sus llaveros, era una muchacha coja, traqueteada en el esqueleto de madera en que se apoyaba. Cuando llegaron se recostaba en la puerta, y su sola pierna ceñida por una media color remedaba la cola de una sirena de arenal fangoso. Cantaba. Y Olaya entró en la glorieta apretado con la mantenedora de la pitahaya, predominando el temblor visible del miedo sobre el escalofrío secreto del placer. El canto de la sirena fangosa se fue hundiendo junto con la argolla de las llaves. Al salir el recuerdo de la sirena ingurgitó, pero ambos juraron que le pondrían un pie encima" (110–11; A26).

The association of the siren or mermaid with mud and a lame girl implies some spiritual defect, a negative aspect that Alberto and his companion resolve to overcome. There is an evolution of sexual relationships in this chapter, which begins with Aredo, Fibo, and his diabolical pencil, progresses to Alberto in the shower and on to his night with the girl, and continues with Alberto serving as a point of contact between his sister Rialta and José Eugenio. While in the shower Alberto dreams of seeing José Eugenio pouring water into a pitcher, that is, of giving form to primal instincts. The budding relationship between José Eugenio and Rialta represents a fruitful manifestation of sensuality, which contrasts with the negative connotations of earlier events.

Although these summaries of metonymic chains in chapters 4 and 5 of *Paradiso* leave out many links, the essential outlines have been presented in the figures cited. The network of associations established in these chapters extends and radiates in all directions throughout the novel.

The power of the mythological figure Angra Mainyu, who is a generator of evil forces and a key element during Alberto's adventure in the showers, is manifested in cold and insects. In

Persian mythology, Angra Mainyu is credited with the creation of all insects harmful to man and plants; cold in this mythological system is regarded as the origin of evil. In the shower episode Angra Mainyu is associated with death, and mention is made of the deity's ability to delay crops. Some of these connotations appear in the classroom scene in which Fibo jabs Aredo. They are also echoed when, during a language lesson, the teacher writes the principal parts of an English verb on the blackboard: "freeze, froze, frozen" (90, 82). This action intensifies Fibo's aggressiveness, because he associates the verb with snow, which suggests to him Aredo's white skin and inactivity. While Fibo's reaction to the verb is to associate it with Aredo, the reader tends to link the concepts of cold and evil. The reader has been prepared for this connection by the passage delineating José Eugenio's perception of Fibo on their way to school on opening day—Fibo's demeanor is compared to that of a person outfitting an iceberg.

Cold usually has negative connotations in *Paradiso*. At the end of chapter 3, the death of Rialta's grandmother "ocupaba en la imaginación familiar la misma extensión terrible de las escarchadas nochebuenas de Jacksonville" (68; A27). In another pathetic episode, the robust Colonel (José Eugenio Cemí) tries to cure his sickly son's asthma by placing him in a bathtub filled with ice. The experiment causes his son to lose consciousness. In a touch of ironic humor, the scene is described as having "algo de los antiguos sacrificios. Sólo que el jefe no sabía a qué divinidad lo ofrecía" (142; A28).

The Colonel's son, José Cemí, is the central character in the novel. One of the greatest sufferings he has to endure is his constant battle with asthma—his struggle to breathe during an attack is in a literal since, a fight for existence. In a vivid description of one asthmatic seizure, the illness is referred to as a divine enemy, which acts like a fly expanding on his chest: "Acarició, bruñéndola de nuevo, las arrugas de la camisa, sintiendo el crecimiento de su jadeo respiratorio, mientras su enemiga divinidad, el asma, se posaba, como una mosca gigante sobre su pecho, y allí comenzaba a zarandearse, a reírse, a engordar con tal rapidez, que sentía una opresión mucho mayor que toda la resistencia de su cuerpo para enfretarla burlarla'' (159–60; A29). The reference to asthma as a "divine enemy"is indicative of the negative forces that José has to wrestle with as his destiny unfolds. Like Alberto, his triumphs and defeats are at times compared to struggles with the gods, who are manifestations of mankind's creativity and, paradoxically, arbiters of his fate.

The associations with flies change as the novel progresses. Flies initially appear in a negative context—one that is based on factual reality. In later references, however, the concept is used in a context that has a cultural basis. In the first chapter, Don María Cemí, José's paternal grandfather (José Eugenio's father), is terrified by stories of crops being destroyed by black flies. This fear causes him to have nightmares of a fly growing inside him. Later in the text, the mythological figure Angra Mainyu appears, and the association of flies with destructive deities is developed. One can surmise that this progression in the text parallels a historical and cultural development in human experience. People confronted the destruction of crops by insects, a process that terrified them, and created a mythological explanation to explain the phenomenon. Associations based on these explanations were then used to create figures that expressed terror. In *Paradiso* the progression moves from the factual to the semiotic as the designation becomes part of a cultural creation. In the case of José, an insect is used to convey the terror of asthma.

There are other dangers in the world besides illness, and, like his father, José is first exposed to the perils of sexuality when he attends school. José Eugenio's experiences in chapters 4 and 5 parallel and complement the events of chapters 8 and 9, which take place while his son José is in school. Chapter 8 mainly concerns manifestations of unbridled sexuality. In a substitution based on the associative links we have been considering, "araña abultada" (217; swollen spider) refers to a woman's sexual organ.

Eco, in his discussion of a model of a communicative system, points out that "the model, in its complexity, is based upon a process of *unlimited semiosis*. Starting with a sign that is considered as a 'type,' one can retraverse, from the center, the extreme periphery, the entire universe of cultural units. Each of these can in turn become the center and generate infinite peripheries."[16] This description closely parallels the sensations one experiences in pursuing the associative links that Lezama Lima has established as a basis for his creation of metaphors. *Paradiso* is a vast network of metonymic chains—a network that generates rich and challenging metaphors. Because the network exists, one section can reverberate throughout the entire system. We have examined only a small segment of this multidimensional network. Using "playa negra" as a point of departure for our examination of this creative process, we have examined the metaphor as an independent entity, as a unit in an individual sentence, and as part of the network. The initial point of contact is necessarily arbitrary; the study could just as well have centered on a number of other figures. However, once a connection has been established, a network of associative links extends in all directions.

Metaphor in *Paradiso* often rests on a metonymic chain, as Lezama Lima combines metaphoric and metonymic processes in his creation of poetic figures. Indeed, this combination is one of the most important features of this remarkable novel. The same process also plays a significant role in much of Lezama Lima's poetry. In "Rapsodia para el mulo," for example, many metaphors are based on metonymical associations with the mule, and in "Los fragmentos de la noche," the sea carries out the same function. Lezama Lima uses metaphor in his works to establish correspondences between individual objects, and metonomy reveals relations based on contiguity. The metonymical mode calls attention to the differences between things, but a shift to metaphor shows that a number of similarities actually unite entities that at first appeared to be separated by time and space. Lezama Lima continually fluctuates between an apprehension of the world that is based on the similarities of metaphor and a perception founded on the contact of metonymy. His employment of these figures is based on a conviction that figurative language can reveal the

16. Eco, *Role of the Reader*, 89.

nature of all things. Metaphor and metonymy are also integral to his quest for identity, as they enable him to understand how individual objects can be related or integrated into major natural or cultural referents.

In *Paradiso* he combines these artistic strategies with his interest in narrative linearity by using his family history as the basis of the story. The incorporation of autobiographical sources is discussed in Chapter 5. The chapter following this one concentrates on Lezama Lima's concept of characterization and on his occasional technique of portraying characters as metaphors as they move between time-bound and time-free states.

3

The Paradigm of Characterization

In describing how he came to the conclusion that a novel can be an extension of poetry, Lezama Lima also explained how he discovered that characters can function as metaphors. "Yo no me puedo considerar, no me he considerado nunca, un novelista. El poema siempre ha sido mi forma de expresión; pero llegó un momento en que vi que el poema se habitaba, que el poema se iba configurando en novela, que había personajes que actuaban en la vida como metáforas, cómo imágenes; vi cómo se entrelazaban, cómo se unían, cómo se diversificaban y entonces comprendí que el poema podía extenderse como novela y que en realidad toda gran novela era un gran poema"[1] (A30). His observations on characterization bring to mind significant questions concerning the relationship between plot and characters and the importance of time in the function of these components.

Time is one of the fundamental preoccupations of twentieth-century art. In literary analysis this concern has been manifested by the stress that has been placed on the ordering of events in narrative. The emphasis on temporal sequence has led to many important discoveries—in works as diverse as those of Vladimir Propp and Gérard Genette[2]—but it has also resulted in a tendency to view important narrative components like characters as mere functions of plot. Seymour Chatman has pointed out that "it is remarkable how little has been said about the theory of character in literary history and criticism."[3] However, a shift in emphasis is beginning to take

1. "Interrogando a Lezama Lima," in *Recopilación de textos sobre José Lezama Lima*, ed. Pedro Simón Martínez, 26.
2. Propp, *Morphology of the Folktale;* Genette, *Figures, Figures II, Figures III.* A part of *Figures III* is available in English in his *Narrative Discourse.*
3. Chatman, *Story and Discourse,* 107.

place. Cesare Segre indicates that the role of characters in a narrative can be regarded in a new light. He notes that in the works of Propp and Claude Bremond, events predominate over characters and "the character continues to be qualified by the actions he performs or is subjected to, by movements he sets in motion or by which he is swept along. In my opinion (and especially when there are in question texts with a marked degree of literary responsibility) these relationships ought, rather, to be inverted: an action interests in the measure in which it reflects the intentions and will of a character. . . . The character, finally, effects a unification of functions, since these make sense because they are carried out by him, fanning out from him."[4] Clearly, Segre questions the importance of the event in the interaction between character and action and disagrees with the subordination of character to plot.

Chatman argues that in many modern works character is supreme and plot is derivative. His point seems well taken, as one can cite examples from Spanish American fiction—such as Guillermo Cabrera Infante's *Tres tristes tigres* and many of the stories of José Agustín—as well as Lezama Lima's *Paradiso,* to support his contention. Yet Chatman claims that attempts to determine whether plot or character is dominant, are not meaningful; existents (characters and setting) and events are both essential components of the narrative, and one should not be subordinated to the other. Chatman's arguments about the question of the dominance of plot or character are meant in a general and theoretical sense. However, a distinction in this matter can be pertinent and useful when applied to individual works.

Although Chatman is well-versed in contemporary intellectual trends (his *Story and Discourse* is a structuralist approach to plot and discourse theory), a good portion of his discussion is focused on the traditional concept of traits and on their use in the creation of characters. "I argue—unoriginally but firmly—for a conception of characters as a paradigm of traits; 'trait' in the sense of 'relatively stable or abiding personal quality,' recognizing that it may either unfold, that is, emerge earlier or

4. Segre, *Structures and Time,* 34.

later in the course of the story, or that it may disappear and be replaced by another. In other words, its domain may end. . . . At the same time, traits must be distinguished from more ephemeral psychological phenomena, like feelings, moods, thoughts, temporary motives, attitudes, and the like. These may or may not coincide with traits."[5]

The distinction between ephemeral psychological phenomena and traits is essentially temporal and is primarily a distinction between transient moods or feelings and persistent characteristics. A character's sudden outburst of rage may be caused by a particular event: the discovery, for example, that he has been swindled out of a sum of money. This character could be said to be angry, but this anger could not be characterized as a trait. On the other hand, if a character frequently becomes angry over trivial matters, the character could be seen as being quick to anger, which is a trait.

Chatman further explains his conception of a "paradigm of traits" by stating: "The paradigmatic view of characters sees the set of traits, metaphorically, as a vertical assemblage intersecting the syntagmatic chain of events that comprise the plot."[6] When he speaks of the "syntagmatic chain of events," he means the fixed linear order of events in a literary work. Events occur in a set order, either in the text or in the reader's reconstruction of the story. Events are subject to cause-and-effect relationships, which exist within a given temporal span. Traits, however, are not time-bound the way events are, and they can exist throughout and beyond a work. "Unlike events, traits are not in the temporal chain, but coexist with the whole or a large portion of it. Events travel as vectors, 'horizontally' from earlier to later. Traits on on the other hand, extend over the time spans staked out by events. They are *parametric* to the

---

5. Chatman, *Story and Discourse*, 126.

6. Ibid., 127. Chatman makes an important distinction between his use of *paradigm* in *Story and Discourse* and its use in linguistics. He points out that in structural linguistics a term appears in a given position "in the absence of, indeed, in opposition to the totality of others that could potentially fill the position it occupies" (ibid.). In literature, however, there is an evocation of other possibilities: "In short, the trait praradigm, like the poetic paradigm, but unlike the linguistic paradigm tends to operate *in praesentia*, not *in absentia*" (ibid., 127–28).

event chain. The communication of existents is not tied rigorously to the chrono-logic, as are the events."[7]

Chatman's distinction between traits and events recalls Lezama Lima's description of his discovery that characters can be viewed as metaphors. In Lezama Lima's view, characters exist within a network of relationships and events, but they emerge from these webs as metaphors or images. Roland Barthes points out that as a reader proceeds through a text, he struggles to name the traits of a character—a process Barthes refers to as a "metonymic skid."[8] According to Chatman, "The motive for 'skidding' is the search for the key to the character, the exact combination of trait-names to sum him up."[9] Barthes indicates that the process is erratic and involves continual self-correction, as multiple possibilities are explored and tested.[10]

The process of discovering traits, as presented in these descriptions, is strikingly similar to mechanisms considered in the study of metaphoric and metonymic modes in Chapter 2. Metaphors and traits are both vertical extensions, although their foundations are different—traits are built upon a syntagmatic process, while metaphors are based on metonymic associations. The processes are most likely interdependent at times. As Chatman states, "The story structure (of which characters are a part), the discourse structure, and the manifestation structure achieve interdependence only because they are independently systematic."[11] A narrative statement can deal with both events and existents at the same time, but "It is only the *because* element that belongs in the event chain."[12]

Lezama Lima's conception of characters as metaphors implies that they are not linked to specific time frames. In many of the unusual episodes in *Paradiso*, time disappears, for the narration either focuses on a character's particular traits or treats him or her as a metaphor. In either case, the result is that

7. Ibid., 129.
8. Barthes, *S/Z*, 92.
9. Chatman, *Story and Discourse*, 134.
10. Barthes, *S/Z*, 92.
11. Chatman, *Story and Discourse*, 137.
12. Ibid., 130.

the reader experiences the character as a time-free being. In a striking example of this technique, a family member remembers an episode in Alberto's life and draws an analogy that recalls Alberto's propensity for prideful anger: "Cincuenta años después de su muerte la cólera del tío Alberto volvía a surgir de rechazo, al ser comparada con la del duque de Provenza, cuya furia consistía en despedazar el vajillero real, pieza tras pieza"[13](A31). Of particular interest is the dynamic persistence of the trait in the minds of other characters long after Alberto has ceased to exist. This vitality is communicated by a time frame of fifty years, as well as by the use of the imperfect past verb tense. It is also significant that this sentence appears in a passage that is already concerned with time and with characteristics that persist long after an individual's death. Another example of this technique occurs when José recalls his dead father. "Recordó cómo también se decía que su padre se aparecía en El Morro, de noche en el pabellón donde daba su clase, buen cumplidor de su sentido misional aun después de muerto" (258; A32). Again, a time frame that extends beyond death is established, and the imperfect past tense is used to suggest that the trait, a highly developed sense of responsibility, exists within a realm of indefinite boundaries.

José's father and Alberto, his maternal uncle, are influential figures during José's childhood. His father, a successful and dynamic colonel in the Cuban army, is a figure of vitality and strength. The Colonel creates a sense of security and harmony in those around him: "Parecía que su destino era fecundar la alegre unidad y prolongar el instante en que nos es dado contemplar las ruedas de la integración y de la armonía" (36; A33). But his energetic vitality overwhelms his young, asthmatic son, who, on more than one occasion, unsuccessfully attempts to live up to his father's expectations. José's vulnerability to his father's strength is forcefully conveyed in an episode that takes place in a small boat. The Colonel has taken José and a colleague's son on an excursion. José Eugenio

13. Lezama Lima, *Paradiso* (Mexico City: Ediciones Era, 1968), 85. Subsequent quotations are from this edition and are noted in the text. The use of a time frame of fifty years is in itself, an interesting device, since the action of the novel after Alberto's death does not span such a long period.

breathes and exhales the sea air as if he were smoking a cigar, but for José, breathing is a painful struggle. "José Eugenio expansionaba su pecho de treinta años, parecía que se fumaba la brisa marina, dilataba las narices, tragaba una épica cantidad de oxígeno, y luego lo iba lanzando por la boca en lentas humaredas. La tranquilidad y el ingenuo color de las aguas, le despertaba un orgullo gritón, natural y salvaje. Pero enfrente veía a su hijo de cinco años, flacucho, con el costillar visible, jadeando cuando la brisa arreciaba, hasta hacerlo temblar con disimulo, pues miraba a su padre con astucia, para fingirle la normalidad de su respiración" (137; A34).

The Colonel is a decisive man of action, and he has little tolerance or understanding of his son's illness. His frustration moves him to act hastily, and at times the results are nearly disastrous. While in the boat, he places José in the water so he can learn how to swim and supports him with his forefinger. Then, in what seems to be a reversal of Michelangelo's vision of God giving spiritual life to Adam by extending his hand so their fingers can touch, the Colonel withdraws his forefinger.[14] José promptly sinks into the water. After a few anxious minutes, the boy is saved. On another occasion, the Colonel places his son in a bathtub full of ice in an effort to cure the boy's asthma, but it only causes José to lose consciousness. These events have a nightmarish influence on José's imagination and are manifested in dreams and in later episodes in the novel. In addition to appearing vital and energetic, the Colonel emerges from these events marked also by the traits of impatience and impulsiveness.

The Colonel's identity and many of his characteristics are frequently associated with his military career. As a leader of a campaign to eradicate banditry from the Cuban countryside, he is pictured as a virile individual capable of decisive leadership. In one episode he calms his troops' fears of being poisoned by sampling some of the food in a joyful and confident manner. This confident display is representative of one of his most persistent traits: a robust and happy expansiveness that communicates his joy in living. Small details are often

14. Michelangelo Buonarroti, *The Creation of Adam,* in the Sistine Chapel.

used to convey such essences. For example, the Colonel, humming tunes from *The Merry Widow* as he returns home one day, carries a yellow melon tucked under one arm, which contrasts with his green uniform. The focus on the vividness of the colors and the melon's shape transforms the fruit into a symbol of the Colonel's life. "Los treinta y tres años que alcanzó su vida fueron de una alegre severidad, parecía que empujaba a su esposa y a sus tres hijos por los vericuetos de su sangre resuelta, donde todo se alcanzaba por alegría, claridad y fuerza secreta. El melón debajo del brazo era uno de los símbolos más estallantes de uno de sus días redondos y plenarios" (19; A35).

Such descriptions create a chain of associations in the reader's mind. In this case the Colonel's uniform is linked to many of his traits by such a metonymic process. As these associations become identified with the Colonel's characteristics, a paradigmatic set of traits is established—a set of traits that extends beyond the temporal limitations of the Colonel's life. In an episode after his death, the Colonel is evoked in part by focusing on parts of his uniform. Rialta, the Colonel's wife, is watching her three children play jacks. As she joins them, the rhythmic movement of the game produces a hypnotic effect. An imaginative process that oscillates between dispersal and unification is set in motion, and fragments of the Colonel's uniform appear.

> Las losas eran para los cuatro jugadores de yaquis un cristal oscilante, aue se rompía silenciosamente, se unía sin perder su temblor, daba paso a fragmentos de telas militares, precisaba ríspidos tachonazos, botones recién lustrados. Desaparecían esos fragmentos, pero instantáneamente reaparecían, unidos a nuevos y mayores pedazos, los botones iban adquiriendo ibanseries. El cuello de la guerrera se iba almidonando con más precisión y fijeza, esperaba el rostro que lo completaría. Rialta, tranquilamente alucinada, iba aumentando en la progresión de los yaquis, se iba acercando al número doce, como quien adormecida sube una escalera, llevando un vaso de agua con tal seguridad que sus aguas permanecen inmóviles, El contorno del círculo se iba endureciendo, hasta parecer de un metal que se tornaba incandescente. De pronto, una fulguración, como si una nube se rompiese para dar paso a una nueva visión, apareció en las losas apresadas por el círculo la guerrera completa del

Coronel de una amarillo como oscurecido, aunque iba ascendiendo en su nitidez, los botones aun los de los cuatro bolsillos, más brillantes que su cobrizo habitual. (174–75; A36)

This movement from fragmentation to unity momentarily suspends the flow of time. The polished buttons, the fragments of military cloth, and a precisely starched collar bring to mind the Colonel's traits: particularly his orderliness, his discipline, and his sense of duty. The brilliant buttons, the stiff collar, and the yellow tunic convey the Colonel's dynamic and joyful energy, which was always channeled into specific goals. Confronted by her husband's traits in this manner, Rialta becomes overwhelmed by her sense of loss, and the momentary spell is broken. But it is clear that the essences embodied in the Colonel's life transcend his death; the Colonel becomes a metaphor and a time-free being.

Alberto shares some of the Colonel's dynamic qualities, but Alberto's capabilities are never submitted to the discipline that characterizes the Colonel. As a result, while the Colonel can be regarded as a symbol of duty and obedience, Alberto is the incarnation of rebellion. When he is still a young man (chapter 5 of *Paradiso*), he defies the authority of the headmaster; he also spends the night away from home engaging in sexual activities. Such acts of rebellion are not unusual in an adolescent, but Alberto's rebelliousness extends into his adult years, and he becomes a millstone around his family's prideful neck. "Para la dinastía familiar de los Cemí y los Olaya, la pequeña dosis demoníaca de Alberto, era más que suficiente" (180; A37). He often appears at his mother's doorstep, hiccuping from excessive drink, and provokes her neighbors' scornful laughter with his antics.

But Alberto is a harmonious as well as a disharmonious presence in his family. His sisters regard him as the "arquetipo de la hombría elegante, el escogido, el arriesgado, el galante, el deseñoso" (182; A38); his mother declares: "Alberto cuando está en calma tiene una alegría que a todos nos fortalece" (191; A39). Joy is associated with both Alberto and the Colonel. They are also both characterized by their smoking mannerisms. Alberto is often seen smoking; the references to the clouds of smoke that accompany him and to the glowing coals of his cigarettes create a vivid image of this formidable character who initiates so much, whose influence is so unsettling. In one instance his cigar is a clarinet, and in another the smoke that envelopes him becomes a suit of armor. "El humo le ha ido fabricando un contorno como si fuese una armadura que ciñe con sus metales esmerilados la congelada niebla marina" (78; A40). In this and other references, the action of smoking becomes an indicator of Alberto's personality. In one example, his presumptuous attitudes are conveyed by his smoking: Alberto "encendía su cigarrillo y lanzaba una presuntuosa primera bocanada" (112; A41). In many instances smoking becomes a character's way of imposing his will on his environment and of marking it with his presence and personality.

This association of the act of smoking with a character's dominance over circumstance is later linked to José.

> Estaba mucho tiempo sentado en su cuarto de estudio, viendo desfilar como un tiro al blanco, la punta encendida de sus cigarros. Contemplaba las chispas, pero no las avivaba, de tal manera que eran frecuentes las veces que las cerillas le quemaban los dedos, mientras la lumbre debilitada por el grosor de las cenizas terminaba por extinguirse en la alianza de la humedad de la saliva con el rescoldo invasor.
> El ejercicio de la poesía, la búsqueda verbal de finalidad desconocida, le iban desarrollando una extraña percepción por las palabras que adquieren un relieve animista en los agrupamientos espaciales, sentadas como sibilas en una asamblea de espíritus. (376–77; A42)

The movement from cigars to contemplation and then to poetry is not a casual progression, for it indicates the path that José eventually takes in his effort to understand and organize his world. Unlike the Colonel and Alberto, who resort to action and extroverted theatrics to impose their will on their environment, José employs more introverted and creative means. But in all three cases, smoking is a sign of the imposition of order and of the human will's attempts to dominate circumstances.

When the narrator first introduces Alberto, he is a child and is peering into the darkness of the night with a pair of naval binoculars. Using his brother's violin as a guitar, he then plays and sings, thereby provoking the complaints of unappreciative neighbors. These two acts, which can be classified as characterizing actions, underscore much of Alberto's importance and function in the novel. He is using the binoculars to increase what little illumination exists in the night and to penetrate the darkness—an act that reduces space and separation. His impromptu musical performance disturbs the neighbors; the incident is a manifestation of the capacity of creativity to upset the existing equilibrium. Alberto has a dual function in *Paradiso;* he is at once a unifying and a disruptive force. For example, it is Alberto who introduces his sister Rialta to her future husband, the Colonel, and likewise it is Alberto who makes their son, José Cemí, aware of the potentialities of language.

During a family reunion, José has the opportunity to listen to a letter that his Uncle Alberto has sent to a member of the family. Demetrio, who reads the letter, tells José: "Acércate más para que puedas oir bien la carta de tu tío Alberto, para que lo conozcas más y le adivines la alegría que tiene. Por primera vez vas a oir el idioma hecho naturaleza, con todo su artificio de alusiones y cariñosas pedanterías" (183; A43). The letter is a tour de force of symbolic and oblique language, in which the real and imagined dangers of the world are defamiliarized and expressed in terms of sea imagery. Alberto's role as an entertainer and as a banisher of boredom is most evident here. The letter, or the potentialities of language it presents, is an absolute revelation to José: "Algo fundamental había sucedido y llegado hasta él. Se le borró, como si hubiese recibido un arponazo de claridad, el concepto familiar del demonismo de Alberto" (185; A44). The metaphorical reference to being struck by "un arponazo de claridad" (a harpoon of clarity) is based on the metonymic links established by Alberto's letter, but it is also another of the many associations with the sea that appear in the context of the strange and the marvelous.

Alberto and the Colonel constitute a duality that greatly influences José. One offers discipline and order, and the other, the excitement of rebellion—two important components of the creative process. Lezama Lima was aware of these functions; he stated that the two characters offer, in rudimentary form, the foundation for poetic expression.[15] There are a number of other binary relationships that also have an important bearing on José's development: his friends Fronesis and Foción, who are decisive during his adolescence; and his mother and Oppiano Licario—spiritual mentors who guide him to manhood and to his dedication to creative writing. The components in these combinations are not always fixed; these relationships are in a state of flux and are sometimes interchangeable. For example, at one point José realizes that his Uncle Alberto and Fronesis play similar roles in his development because they both sought him out.

Lezama Lima created dualities in *Paradiso*—such as distance and proximity, the real and the unreal—that, in his view, give the novel "an inextinguishable rhythm."[16] Relationships are also crucial to the work because of their importance in the determination of character. Lezama Lima took great care to place the characters in *Paradiso* within networks of family and cultural traditions. He conceived his characters as points that move through complex webs of time and space; as a result, *Paradiso* is a vast configuration of complicated relationships.

As the main character, José Cemí is the central point toward which all movement in *Paradiso* converges. The novel follows him from infancy to young manhood; Therefore it is best to regard him as an entity in formation. He is what Boris Tomashevsky would term a "dynamic character," that is, one whose characteristics are in a state of flux throughout the work,[17] or what E. M. Forster calls a "round" character—one that is unpredictable and full of conflicting traits.[18] Such a character is, in short, capable of change. However, he does acquire a definitive set of traits by the end of the novel.

Although the pairs of characters that are important in Cemí's life usually represent opposites, they also share important

15. "Eran hombres en que la poesía penetraba y salía, pero no iban a la gravitación del poema" (Lezama Lima, *Cartas*, 95).

16. Lezama Lima, *Cartas*, 94.

17. Tomashevsky, "Thematics," in *Russian Formalist Criticism*, ed. and trans. Lee T. Lemon and Marion J. Reis, 89.

18. Forster, *Aspects of the Novel*, as quoted in Chatman, *Story and Discourse*, 131–32.

characteristics. In the case of his father and his uncle, the two men are both dynamic extroverts who radiate a positive and happy view of life. Although Fronesis and Foción are very different, they have similar problems—family difficulties and sexual maladjustments. Fronesis, through ritualistic and creative means, overcomes his inability to have sexual relations with a woman. Foción never resolves his bisexuality, and his inability to impose order on his inner turmoil leads to an emotional breakdown.[19] One friend is overwhelmed by chaotic forces, but the other succeeds in controlling those that threaten him. Their actions serve as examples of the positive and negative resolution of dangerous struggles; they also operate as models. José reveals himself not only in what he decides to do but also, more importantly, in what he avoids. In this regard, aspects of his characterization are very indirect.[20]

José's relationship with the Colonel is particularly revealing; it makes José's physical inadequacies more obvious. The asthmatic, timid, and introverted son cannot hope to duplicate or match the dynamic and decisive activity of his robust father. Although José frequently attempts to fulfill his father's expectations by ignoring his body's negative reactions to physical challenges, such episodes end in minor disasters—much to the consternation of both father and son. But José possesses a vivid imagination, and his impressive experiences often find expression in dreams. In one nightmare, in which a number of associations are established between the son and his father, José is described as an "infantil general de tropas invisibles" (152; "infant general of invisible troops," 140). Through a process that involves advice from friends and family members as well as direct experience, José begins to realize that the Colonel's adventurous spirit can find expression through him by intellectual means.

Ten years after the Colonel's unexpected death at the age of thirty-three, José returns home one day after having participated in a political demonstration. His mother is relieved that

---

19. A discussion of these struggles and the imagery used to convey them is contained in Raymond D. Souza, *Major Cuban Novelists*, 60–65.

20. Tomashevsky discusses direct and indirect characterization in his "Thematics," in *Russian Formalist Criticism*, ed. and trans. Lemon and Reis, 88.

he is safe and tells him that she had been thinking seriously about him and his father. She links the two by pointing out: "Todo lo que tu padre no pudo realizar, tú lo vas haciendo a través de los años, pues en una familia no puede suceder una desgracia de tal magnitud, sin que esa oquedad cumpla una extraña significación, sin que esa ausencia vuelva por su rescate" (245; A45). She continues linking father and son and tells José:

> No rehuses el peligro, pero intenta siempre lo más difícil. Hay el peligro que enfrentamos como una sustitución, hay también el peligro que intentan los enfermos, ese es el peligro que no engendra ningún nacimiento en nosotros, el peligro sin epifanía. Pero cuando el hombre, través de sus días ha intentado lo más difícil, sabe que ha vivido en peligro, aunque su existencia haya sido silenciosa, aunque la sucesión de su oleaje haya sido manso, sabe que ese dí que a que le ha sido asignado para su transfigurarse, verá, no los peces dentro del fluir, lunarejos en la movilidad, sino los peces en la canasta estelar de la eternidad. (245–46; A46)

Rialta's statements to her son encourage him to develop his own characteristics, but within the tradition represented by his father. The Colonel's vitality had been directed against the dangers of the physical world, but she urges José to struggle against other perils. Possibly sensing that her son has not overcome the imposing shadow of his father, she suggests that he follow a family tradition by not avoiding risks and challenges and by attempting the most difficult. Such endeavors, she clearly indicates, can take place in intellectual as well as physical realms. The dangers are great, but the fear of failure must be overcome if permanent accomplishments ("the fish in the starry basket of eternity") are to be achieved. The importance of Rialta's words cannot be overestimated, because they are central to what José is to become.

Rialta's role as a spiritual mentor is reinforced at the end of the novel by Oppiano Licario, who intensifies José's introduction into the mysterious struggles of creativity. Licario is the bridge linking José to his family and to his destiny as a writer, and he seems to always appear during significant events in José's family. Licario helps Alberto avoid danger on his first night away from home, and he is present at the Colonel's death. Also, Licario's presence is instrumental in helping José overcome the trauma of his father's demise. At the end of *Paradiso*, Licario indicates to José that he has successfully surmounted many dangers and that he is ready to deal with the challenges of creative activities. José's contacts with Licario at this point have all the connotations of a ritualistic initiation, and these events mark José's passage through a special threshold: the commitment to creative writing. This decision is presented as a great adventure and is communicated by actions and symbols generally associated with the hero archetype.[21]

José's mother and Oppiano Licario nurture some of the young man's most promising traits, particularly those associated with his father and his uncle. José tempers the Colonel's vitality with his own patience and Alberto's rebellious creativity with disciplined observation. José is encouraged to foster these tendencies and to use these traits in developing his own unique expression. In this respect, José becomes a synthesis of traditions—which pertain to his family—and his own individuality.

By this point in the novel, José has a specific paradigm of traits. He is secure because he possesses a sense of his roots, belongs to a specific time and place, has overcome the turmoil of adolescence, and has found a destiny. He seeks unity in diversity and is as interested in the small details of existence as in theoretical concepts. He is intellectually curious, patient, observant, and, due to his asthma, physically tense and inactive. Above all, he is imaginative and committed to writing. He regards creativity as a way to knowledge because the creative act involves the unification of diverse and often unseen or unnoticed elements, and to see is to know. Significantly, creativity is also a means to overcome the tedium and boredom of life.

As the novel progresses, José's imagination becomes more important; indeed it seems likely that his creative thought transforms sections of the text. This possibility is explored in the next chapter of this study, but it is of more than passing interest to note here the prospect of such a dialectic, since

21. See Joseph Campbell, *The Hero with a Thousand Faces.*

José's imaginative faculties constitute one of the more intriguing components in his paradigm of traits. The events in the novel are time-bound, but the traits associated with José are essentially time-free. Although the character José Cemí is created in part through his own actions as well as by direct characterization on the part of the narrator and other personages in the novel, the characterization is accomplished largely by indirect means. For this reason, the categorization of relationships is as important in the understanding of a character as are the mechanisms that create a trait or a metaphoric concept of a character.

In a perceptive discussion of characterization, Leon Surmelian wrote that "a character in fiction is a synthesis of diverse elements and the result of the same unifying inner vision that sees the like in the unlike and draws the fragments together like a magnet."[22] His comments are not only apropos to characterization in *Paradiso*, but also to the general creative process of this novel, because, in its creation, Lezama Lima frequently considered a number of widely separated factors and united them into a cohesive whole. This process was used in the creation of traits. But Lezama Lima also took characters and events that are separated in time and space and telescoped them into a unified view of reality. A movement from fragmentation to unity occurs as the pieces of different mosaics swirl into place. In this manner, Lezama Lima conveyed his conviction that order and unity do exist in the world—although they are not always apparent. Lezama Lima's interest in the achievement of unity is related to his desire to overcome the barriers of time, to reach a state that is time-free. Lezama Lima's belief that characters can be considered metaphors indicates that he was aware of the syntagmatic and paradigmatic functions of language. And his conception of characterization is intimately related to the way that metonymy and metaphor operate in his works. In both cases, linear and time-bound function became the basis for a time-free creation; these mechanisms provided a basis for the expression of his quest for eternity.

22. Surmelian, *Techniques of Fiction Writing*, 140.

4

Organizational Configurations: Plot and Fabula

It is usually assumed that the presentation of events in *Paradiso* generally follows a traditional chronological pattern, with the main episodes of the novel taking place between the waning years of the nineteenth century and the fourth decade of the present. This is essentially correct, but there are some marked temporal dislocations in *Paradiso,* and chapter 12 contains the most challenging ones. This chapter constitutes a complete break with the chronological ordering that preceeds it and, at first glance, seems far removed from the contents of the other chapters. There are four separate story lines in the chapter, and they are presented in alternating sections. The beginnings of all the stories are told first; then the sequence of stories is repeated as the second and third sections are related. The stories merge in the fourth segment—mainly through the overlapping of central figures. This occurs despite the separations of time and space that divide the four narrations.[1] The first story relates the exploits of a Roman military tribune, and while the other three stories take place in Havana and are contemporary to most of the events in *Paradiso,* none of the characters in these stories seems to be related in any way to the characters presented in the first eleven chapters. The chapter closes with a vignette in which two centurions play a game of dice at the ruins of a Christian temple that is built over the remnants of an academy for pagan philosophers. Chapter 12 is a very expansive section of the novel; its unexpected appearance challenges the reader but also raises serious questions about the unity of the work. In order to gain some insight into the importance and function of this unusual section, some of

1. A more detailed summary and analysis of the chapter's contents is available in Raymond D. Souza, *Major Cuban Novelists,* 66–71.

the organizational patterns that exist in the novel will be examined in order to see if chapter 12 fits into the overall design of *Paradiso* and to see if there are any correspondences between elements in chapter 12 and those in other sections of *Paradiso*. In considering this issue, the distinction between plot and story—an analytical concept first used by the Russian Formalists—will be employed.

Although the Russian Formalist movement existed for only a short time (approximately 1915–1930), its influence on the development of literary theory in this century has been decisive; literary critics are still in the process of working out the implications of many of the Russian Formalists' discoveries and preoccupations.[2] One of their fundamental concerns was the difference between plot (*syuzhet*) and story (*fabula*), that is, the difference between the arrangement of the contents of a narrative as encountered in a text (plot) and its rearrangement in chronological order (story). This distinction has been the origin of many insights, but it has also engendered a good deal of confusion. In applying the concept, critics have employed diverse terminologies and have used varying levels of abstraction. Cesare Segre points out that this dichotomy is referred to as *discours* and *histoire* by Todorov, *récit* and *histoire* by Genette, and as *récit racontant* and *récit raconté* by Bremond.[3] Other examples can be cited—such as Seymour Chatman's use of story (content) and discourse (expression) and Meir Sternberg's complicated model of eight possible combinations based on his concepts of story, fabula, plot, and sujet.[4] The

---

2. For a detailed study of the movement, see Victor Erlich, *Russian Formalism*. A briefer analysis is available in Spanish in Renato Prada Oropeza, *La autonomía literaria* (Jalapa, Mexico: Centro de Investigaciones Lingüístico-Literarias, 1977). The connections between formalism and structuralism are well delineated in Fernande M. DeGeorge, "From Russian Formalism to French Structuralism." Essays by the formalists are available in Lee T. Lemon and Marion J. Reis, eds. and trans., *Russian Formalist Criticism;* Ladislav Matejka and Krystyna Pomorska, eds., *Readings in Russian Poetics;* and Tzvetan Todorov, ed., *Teoría de la literatura de los formalistas rusos*.

3. Segre, "Analysis of the Tale, Narrative Logic, and Time," in his *Structures and Time,* 1.

4. Chatman, *Story and Discourse;* and Sternberg, *Expositional Modes and Temporal Ordering in Fiction*.

terminology will undoubtedly continue to change as new concepts evolve and different methodologies are developed. Segre's essay offers a positive contribution to this process: he reviews the origin and evolution of the concept from the Russian Formalists on and clarifies the many challenges involved in applying the theory.

Segre uses four categories in his own analysis: discourse, plot, fabula, and narrative model.[5] Discourse refers to the narrative text as signifier, plot to the sum of content units corresponding to the discourse level or to these units in the order they are encountered in the text, fabula to the content units reorganized into logical temporal order, and narrative model to the abstract underlying design or deep structure. One of the many advantages of Segre's scheme is that it moves from the specific to the abstract. By beginning with discourse, he first presents the most concrete category: the words and sentences of the text. In his discussion of the relationship between discourse and plot, Segre points out that the reader of a book cannot read more than one sentence at a time.[6] As a

5. Segre points out:

> The uncertainty of the terminology, aggravated by the now habitual *analyse du récit* in place of 'analysis of the fabula,' derives from the fact that a mere dichotomy is inadequate to represent the field of research effectively. Plot and fabula are in reality two ways of representing content, while what is lacking is a term which will indicate its signifying aspect. Thus I shall adopt, at least at the outset, a three-part division: *discourse* (the narrative text as signifier), *plot* (textual content in the order of its presentation), and *fabula* (content or, better, its cardinal elements, as rearranged in logical and chronological order). (Segre, *Structures and Time*, 1–2)

He then adds a fourth category—narrative model—which denotes the most abstract level. Segre clarifies the processes of formalistic criticism by pointing out the different ways critics regard various categories or move from one to another. He notes, for example, that Shklovsky and Tomashevsky see plot as the same, but that their concepts of fabula fluctuate between his ideas of fabula and narrative model. Propp, on the other hand, directly contrasts plot and narrative model, since folk narration has few temporal displacements.

6. Segre notes: "The reader of a book *at any given moment reads no more than a single sentence;* all those that preceded it have been built into a memorial synthesis (of subject matter, stylistic elements, allusions), while those which remain to be read form an area of potentiality in both linguistic and narrative terms" (Ibid., 11). Such a process is possible because "it is the genetic integra-

result, it is impossible to achieve a stylistic or linguistic analysis of a text's temporal axis. In the process of reading, the reader disregards the temporal or linear order of the story and instead constructs various paradigms. Segre delineates two kinds of "summarizing paraphrase[s]": The first (plot) accepts all the temporal and spatial dislocations in the text, while the second (fabula) rearranges things in chronological order.[7] However, since it is impossible to reproduce every element encountered in the text, it is necessary to paraphrase or synthesize, and therefore the reader, while accepting the plot, must also abstract it.

A comparison of plot and fabula is important to an understanding of the dislocations and organizational strategies used in a work. In order to arrive at a satisfactory understanding of these elements, the discourse has to be analyzed by dividing it into segments.[8] In the following examination of the organizational patterns in *Paradiso*, two types of linear ordering are

---

tion of content and expression that makes it possible to carry through as a unity a reading apparently split up in this manner: in the overall complexity of a work, its formal elements play a fundamental role in defining content also" (Ibid., 12).

7. Ibid., 15.

8. According to Segre the process of segmentation should have "at least two main objectives: (1) to prepare sequences which, rearranged in terms of content chronology, will constitute the fabula and (2) to arrive at zones of convergence between various types of discourse function and various types of language. In other words, there is a linear segmentation and a segmentation into linguistic and functional classes" (Ibid., 17). After pointing out that in linear segmentation, segments are usually brought to an end by digressions or by forward- or backward-looking segments, he notes:

> The interest of linear segmentation lies in its *impossibility*. Linear segmentation brings us into contact with 'cross-reference segments,' those which assure the text's intelligibility over and above the temporal movement to and fro actuated within it. And it is not simply a matter of bracketing 'cross-reference segments' in order to make possible a rearrangement of the fabula: backward- and forward-looking segments for the most part take on particular modes of exposition—speech, soliloquy, dream, presentiment, etc. (in the case of characters)—insertion, foreshadowing, etc. (in the technique of narrative discourse). This is why the fabula can be formulated only in summary form which changes the way in which the events are formulated, a fact which confirms what has

noted—one that has its basis in events and another that is based on two characters, the Colonel and his son José. This segmentation most likely involves a greater degree of abstraction than that intended by Segre, since it focuses mainly on major narrative units. Therefore it is important to keep in mind Segre's statement: "Fabula is always a summary; but the sum of the motivations is so complex that only the text in its entirety can indicate it. The text remains impregnable to our attacks; our most striking success can be only to make it speak to us."[9] In diagram A, a comparison of the plot and the fabula in the first six chapters, as represented in major narrative units, reveals some interesting patterns.

Diagram A

Chapter	I	II	III	IV	V	VI
Plot summary	José's asthma attack, family's conflict with cook	José's youth, Colonel's trips to Jamaica and Mexico	Rialta's youth, her family history	Colonel's youth, his family history	Colonel and Alberto in school, Alberto's rebellion, Colonel and Rialta meet	Colonel and Rialta's courtship and first years of marriage, Colonel's attempts to cure José, Colonel's death in Pensacola
Fabula	5	7	1	2	3	4 6 8

---

already been noted, that the fabula is primarily an instrument for measuring deviations from the order of narrative succession. (Ibid., 18)

Segre recognizes the degree of summary and abstraction that takes place in formulating the fabula and, interestingly enough, notes that cross-reference segments can be tied to narrative discourse or characters.
9. Ibid., 21.

What is most apparent is the number of time dislocations in chapter 6 and the use of the chapter as the focal point or touchstone of the novel's action, which moves back and forth in time throughout the text.

When linear ordering is based on the Colonel and José (C and J in diagram B), the same pattern emerges. (J–4 refers to José's presence at his father's death.)

Diagram B

Chapters	I	II	III	IV	V	VI
	C–4	C–6		C–1	C–2	C–3
						C–5
						C–7
	J–1	J–3				J–2
						J–4

Whether the linear chronology is based on narrative units or on the lives of the characters, chapter 6 becomes a focal point. Since linear segmentation is impossible because of cross-references, backward- and forward-looking segments based on such elements as dreams or speeches have been excluded from these diagrams (except for the references to the family histories in chapters 3 and 4). But an examination of cross-references in chapter 6 leads to some interesting conclusions.

Chapter 6 begins with a passage about Grandmother Mela (Rialta's paternal grandmother), in which the ninety-four-year-old woman relives events in her past. One memorable episode takes place during one of Cuba's many struggles for separation from Spain during the nineteenth century. Mela successfully bluffs some loyalist troops and keeps them from searching a henhouse where three hundred rifles are hidden. In the context of chapter 6, this event's remoteness in time is significant. The chapter begins with the most remote event in the first six chapters and closes with the most recent: the death of the Colonel.[10]

Events are presented in chronological order in chapters 7 through 11. Except for dreams, visions, and conversations in which characters relate the pasts of others, the ordering of events closely parallels José's life. Attention is also given to the worldly dangers that surround him, particularly unbridled sexuality and violence. These concerns are developed in chapters 8 and 9—units that have the same significance and function in the telling of José's life that chapters 4 and 5 did in the Colonel's story. In both cases, contacts initiated in school serve as introductions to the evils and dangers of the world.

Chapter 12 represents a complete break with the chronological ordering that preceeds it, and its contents seem far removed from the plot or fabula. Lezama Lima has referred to the chapter as a negation of time through dreams[11]—an interesting description since the segments are not presented like other dreams in the novel. It is not directly apparent that these segments are dreams, although the irrational nature of many of the events and the numerous archetypal allusions are evident. Whether they are dreams or visions is open to question, but it is obvious that the contents of chapter 12 represent a profound transformation of reality, and the segmentation of the chapter is particularly intriguing.

The first story in the chapter narrates the exploits of a Roman military tribune, Atrio Flaminio. Flaminio is an astute and fearless leader who overcomes human and occult forces in his military campaigns, but his fondest wish—to die in battle—is frustrated when he succumbs to an illness. The next three narrations take place in Havana and are generally contemporary to the time of the novel. In the second story, a small child breaks a large vase while under the care of his grandmother, and this event produces a great deal of consternation and fear. The child reappears in the third and fourth stories and serves

10. In chapter 3 reference is made to Doña Augusta's mother (Rialta's maternal grandmother) as "hija de un oidor de la Audencia de Puerto Rico" (50), but it is presented as an evocation of the past rather than as an event.
11. Lezama Lima, *Cartas*, 94.

as one of several elements that unify the four narrations. In the third story, an anonymous individual encounters strange and secret forces in his home and as he wanders through Havana. During one of his walks, he sees a child in a circle but is unable to ascertain who it is. It is later revealed that this child and the one in the second story are the same. The fourth story concerns an old music critic, Juan Longo. (The central character in the first and fourth narrations are given specific names, but all the others are anonymous.) Longo's wife attempts to remove him from time's flow by placing him in a cataleptic trance. After spending some fifty years in a state of suspension, his condition is discovered, and he is placed on public display.

Here the four stories merge as the anonymous individual of the third story peers into Juan Longo's casket and sees the child of the second narration. Also, when Longo's wife looks into the casket, she sees the face of Atrio Flaminio, who is desperately attempting to join his troops. She screams, breaking the suspension of time, and the figures disintegrate as they pass through the whirlwinds of temporality into eternity.

The chapter closes with a vignette in which two centurions play dice among the ruins of a Christian temple, which is located on the former site of an academy for pagan philosophers. The dice are thrown and the numbers two and three appear. The number two most likely stands for duality, while the three denotes synthesis and unity. At this point a bust of a geometrician who is holding a compass falls and strikes the die that shows three, changing the number to two. As a result of this incident, the number symbolism points in two directions. The movement from three to two can be seen as a reversal from synthesis to duality, but if the final total of the dice (four) is considered, the meaning is different. The unity symbolized by three is destroyed in this case as well, and the appearance of four indicates the orderly display of a new form or the manifestation of a tradition dedicated to logic and symmetry. After this event, the two men, covered by a single cape and looking like a turtle, leave the ruins.

The number four appears so many times in the chapter (four stories each divided into four parts, the dice showing four, the four legs of the turtlelike figure of the centurions) that it is probably indicative of "the orderly arrangement of what is separate"[12]—in this case, life and death, time and eternity, and materiality and creativity. The geometrician's compass, an instrument used to draw circles, can be regarded as a synthesis of penetration or insight (the leg of the compass) and incorporation (the circles it draws). The compass is another manifestation of the circle image, which is used frequently in *Paradiso* to convey a process that imposes form over disorder or chaos.[13] Another sign of synthesis is the turtle. Its round upper shell symbolizes heaven, and its lower square (the four legs) represents earth.[14] Even the chapter number suggests the same movement to form, for Cirlot points out that twelve is "symbolic of cosmic order and salvation. . . . Linked to it are the notions of space and time, and the wheel or circle."[15] The association of twelve with time is particularly strong because of the division of a day into two units of twelve hours and the year into twelve months. The frequent appearance of four, particularly in the concluding vignette, indicates a movement toward wholeness and the integration of the four faculties of the mind (intellect, intuition, emotion, and sensation) into a complete personality. Within a sexual code, the number two represents the duality of choice (heterosexual or homosexual); the destruction of the number three by the compass (a synthesis of masculine and feminine symbolism) signifies a banishment of a preoccupation with male sexuality; and four stands for the ordered and harmonious integration of sexual instincts. In this regard, the final episode symbolizes the process a young person (José Cemí) might experience on his journey to adulthood.

The unusual contents of chapter 12 raise serious and challenging questions about the section's relationship to the plot

12. Juan Eduardo Cirlot, *A Dictionary of Symbols*, 225. Lezama Lima has stated that at the end of the chapter, "logro la tetractis, el cuatro, dios" (Lezama Lima, *Las eras imaginarias*, 182).

13. Circle imagery is discussed in Souza, *Major Cuban Novelists*, 58–65; and in his "La imagen del círculo en *Paradiso* de Lezama Lima."

14. Cirlot, *Dictionary of Symbols*, 334.

15. Ibid., 224.

and the fabula of *Paradiso*. One critic, Jaime Valdivieso, has speculated that the symbolic figures in this chapter correspond directly to the novel's characters.[16] Although Valdivieso does not develop this insight or offer conclusive evidence to support his contention, his assertion that correspondences exist between chapter 12 and other sections of the novel is well-founded. However, I would modify his suggestion that one-to-one relationships exist between figures or elements and characters. Some one-to-one symbolic relationships do exist, but, on the whole, I suspect that symbolic relationships more often exist in combinations. When the various characters look into Juan Longo's casket, for example, a definite synthesis of Flaminio, the child, and the music critic takes place. There are also indications that some of the characters are split into more than one entity. The stroller who encounters strange forces, for example, may be attempting to capture his own essence when he sees the child in the circle. When he peers into the casket and confronts the child, this polarization ceases to exist.

In many respects, many of the functions of chapter 6 are duplicated in chapter 12. Both sections begin with events that are far removed in time from the major contents of the chapter, and time and death are central concerns in the two units. This thematic overlap is matched by the correspondence of events concerning the Colonel in chapter 6 and Atrio Flaminio in chapter 12. Both men are dynamic leaders who calm their men's fears during important campaigns, but despite their great vitality and extroverted activities, they die young, defeated by illness. In addition to these direct parallels, the two chapters both operate as magnets, or the focal points of many other sections of the text. The segmentation operates differently for each of the chapters, however. In the case of chapter 6, disruption of temporal sequences occurs between it and other chapters, whereas the process of alternation or segmentation

16. "Y en otro de los capítulos finales aparece [*sic*] una abuela, un niño, un paseante, un músico, un capitán de legiones que pueden ser respectivamente los espíritu [*sic*] del Coronel, José Cemí, la abuela, el músico Squab y Oppiano Licario. También contribuye a esta sincronía la continua repetición de diversos símbolos: la triada, Eros, el círculo, la serpiente, el andrógino, el Hades que representan también la unidad" (Jaime Valdivieso, *Bajo el signo de Orfeo*, 30).

is more internal in chapter 12. Although there are a number of differences in the two chapters, there are enough similarities to suggest that they together serve as important units in the organizational configuration of the novel. The two chapters rely to a great extent on correspondences with elements in other sections of *Paradiso,* and this feature is particularly important to our interpretation of chapter 12.

Victor Shklovsky indicates that as a text is read, segments of it are superimposed on one another. ''The subject (plot) is constituted, via connections between the various parts, by the repetition of the same passages, and these become transcurrent images. . . . When we read a passage, we perceive it against the background of another. We have been given an orientation toward a connection, and we try to interpret it. This modifies our perception of the passage.''[17] This type of connection occurs many times in chapter 12 and can be related to a small detail, an image, or an event. The variety and number of the associations throughout the novel are remarkable. Although these repetitions frequently have symbolic value, some of them are barely noticeable during an initial reading. But there are so many of them that the reader is apt to recognize a few. For example, in both chapters 5 and 6, a compass is hurled against another object. In chapter 2, José casually holds a piece of chalk against a wall while walking—an action that is repeated in chapter 12 by a child with a lump of coal. In the first episode of the novel, three servants who are seeing José through an attack of asthma are apprehensive about the return of the Colonel and his wife, because they do not want to be blamed if anything goes amiss. This motif of fear in connection with the anticipated return of parents is repeated three times in the story in chapter 12 concerning the grandmother and the child.

In chapter 6 a nun who is nicknamed Mary Moon because of her paleness interrupts a fight between José and another child, which occurs just before the Colonel's death. The grandmother of the child in chapter 12 is named María la Luna, and she protects the child from an unnamed danger. As in chapter 6, these events in chapter 12 occur just prior to the appearance of death imagery—in this case in the form of the figures in the coffin. The presence of Atrio Flaminio in the casket recalls three vivid encounters with death that José experiences in chapter 6: Augusta's description of the exhumation of her father, who was buried in a policeman's uniform; José's observation of his father's body in full military dress; and Augusta's admonition to José regarding a wax figure of a saint in a glass case, which she says is real.

The association of wax with death is particularly vivid to José. The connection is established in the following quotation from chapter 6, which, in the Spanish version, contains an autobiographical shift from the third to the first person. "La cera de la cara y de las manos perfeccionaba lo que yo, por indicación de mi Abuela y por desconocimiento de que existiesen esos trabajos en cera, creía que era la verdadera muerte. Que allí no había una imagen siquiera, sino un corrientísimo molde de cera, ni siquiera trabajando con un exceso de realismo que se prestara a la confusión, no podía ser precisado por Cemí, a sus seis años, en que iba descubriendo los objetos, pero sin tener una masa en extenso que fuera propicia a la formación de análogos y a los agrupamientos de las desemejanzas en torno a núcleos de distribución y de nuevos ordenamientos"[18] (A47).

José's association of death with wax and with his grandmother's story of her exhumed father is so great that these connections immediately come to mind when he sees his father's body. "El ordenanza descorrió la sábana. Vio, de pronto, a su padre muerto, ya con su uniforme de gala, los dos brazos cruzados sobre el pecho. La piel no se parecía a la cera que veía en sus pesadillas en el rostro de Santa Flora, que le traía su primer recuerdo de la muerte. Esperó un momento, su padre permanecía inmóvil. No se volatilizaba, como oyó contar a su Abuela que le sucedió a su padre cuando la exhumación. La piel que ya no está recorrida por la sangre, no en la cera

18. Lezama Lima, *Paradiso* (Mexico City: Ediciones Era, 1968), 153. Subsequent quotations are from this edition and are noted in the text.

de la muerte en Santa Flora. No era el remolino del polvo del cuento de su Abuela. Pero allí estaba su padre muerto. El ordenanza volvió a cubrirlo con la sábana" (169; A48). This passage contains a series of transcurrent images that reappear in chapter 12. José's association of the three elements—wax, the whirlwind of dust, and disintegration—with death are echoed in the synthesis and eventual disappearance of the three figures in Juan Longo's casket. Longo's wife, in an effort to protect him from death, coats his body with wax so he will not be consumed by white ants. This use of insects as a manifestation of destruction is consistent with a metonymic chain that extends throughout the text, and the wax and the ants recall the first episode in the novel.

When *Paradiso* opens, José, at five years of age, is suffering an attack of asthma, and angry red welts appear on his body. The woman caring for him, Baldovina, is told by other servants that the child has been bitten by an ant lion. At one point, Baldovina allows drops of sperm-oil wax from a candle to fall on José's body. The welts and the wax drippings on the child's body become metaphors of the struggle between destructive and preservative forces. This dichotomy reappears when José associates his father's body with the wax figure of the saint and also in the efforts of Juan Longo's wife to escape time.

These connections and numerous others contribute to the unity, or cohesion, of the novel. According to M. A. K. Halliday and Ruqaiya Hasan, "The concept of cohesion is a semantic one; it refers to relations of meaning that exist within the text, and that define it as a text. Cohesion occurs when the INTERPRETATION of some element in the discourse is dependent on that of another. The one PRESUPPOSES the other, in the sense that it cannot be effectively decoded except by recourse to it. When this happens, a relation of cohesion is set up, and the two elements, the presupposing and the presupposed, are thereby at least potentially integrated into a text."[19] Halliday and Hasan term "a single instance of cohesion" a *tie*.[20] Many of the correspondences that exist between chapter 12 and other

19. Halliday and Hasan, *Cohesion in English*, 4.
20. Ibid., 3.

sections of *Paradiso* function as ties. This indicates that despite its complexity, chapter 12 is an important component of the novel's meaning.

In chapter 6, when José sees his dead father and thinks of wax, the word *nightmares* is used to convey the impact of the earlier events on his imagination. Lezama Lima has indicated that chapter 12 consists of dreams, but if one is willing to consider this possibility, one has to inquire about the identity of the dreamer. This is an important question in any attempt to explain the relationship of the contents of chapter 12 to the plot and fabula of the novel. At first glance the story concerning Atrio Flaminio seems to be far removed from the rest of the text, but if other cross-reference segments, repetitions, and ties are considered, a semantic pattern emerges.

Many of the episodes that José experiences in the novel are transformed into dreams, and at times the objects that he observes are animated by his imagination. The Colonel's attempt to teach his son how to swim by withdrawing his finger results in many nightmares for José. In another episode in chapter 11, José is engaged in creative writing, and he pauses to meditate on some objects he had seen in a gift shop window. As he thinks of the arrangment he had observed and others he had made himself, he begins to realize that the ordering of objects can constitute a creative act that transcends time and space. "Eso lo llevó a meditar cómo se producían en él esas recomposiciones espaciales, ese ordenamiento de lo invisible, ese sentido de las estalactitas. Pudo precisar que esos agrupamientos eran de raíz temporal, que no tenían nada que ver con los agrupamientos espaciales, que son siempre una naturaleza muerta; para el espectador la fluencia del tiempo convertía esas ciudades espaciales en figuras, por las que el tiempo al pasar y repasar, como los trabajos de las mareas en las plataformas coralinas, formaba como un eterno retorno de las figuras que por estar situadas en la lejanía eran un permanente embrión" (380; A49). In this section of the text, the reader is allowed to enter the mind of a writer engaged in the act of creating. These meditations on time and space are a miniature version of what transpires in chapters 12 and 13.

Of particular significance in the above quotation is the mention of the "eternal return," a reference to the concept of eternal recurrence, which was developed by Friedrich Nietzsche in *Thus Spoke Zarathustra*. In Lezama Lima's text, the idea is presented as an analogy related to an aesthetic arrangement, which suggests that creativity has the ability to defy time. These observations point to the importance of repetition in aesthetic creations and indicate that the reader can expect that some characters and events will repeatedly return as imaginative transformations.

José's ability to re-create and transform his experiences is a key to interpreting chapter 12. Although Flaminio's story seems extraneous to the events in *Paradiso*, it is not the only segment in the novel that deals with the Roman era. In chapter 9 José arrives at the university one morning, where he encounters an atmosphere that is described with references to sexuality and the Roman god Terminus.

> Al día siguiente, al llegar por la mañana a Upsalón, notó en todos los grupos una festinación, una alharaca casi, que interrumpía las clases. La gravedad socarrona del dios Término parecía estar en el centro de esos grupos. Un solo tema levantaba el comento procaz, seudocientífico, libertino o condenatorio. En el centro, el dios Término, con una mandíbula moviente, que remedaba una risa solfeando un solo hecho, con un enorme falo, y en la mano derecha un cuerno. A cada uno de los ascensos y descensos de la mandíbula, correspondía un movimiento rítmico de la mano con el cuerno que tapaba la hímnica longura del falo.
>
> El comentario alegraba todos los grupos en una esperma naciente. Un relator, y luego las variantes y el juego de las invenciones. Cemí recordó que cuando estaba en el castillo de la Fuerza y fue agraciado con una visión de las que él se reía, había situado delfines sobre caballos que corrían sus mutaciones entre el mundo inorgánico y el tétano. Delfines símbolo de un desvío sexual, que retozan cerca de la concha donde la cipriota diosa se envuelve en sus velos de salitre. (259; A50)

José soon discovers that acceptable boundaries of human sexuality have been overstepped and that one of the university's outstanding athletes has been caught engaging in homosexual acts. This event provokes a variety of reactions among the students and a long discussion between José, Fronesis, and Foción on the nature and origin of various stages of sexuality. When he is leaving the university after these events, José experiences a vision of a Roman fertility rite, replete with a number of figures including aristocratic Roman women, virgins, bulls, and an enormous phallus. These transformations of reality take place within the context of dangerous events that involve sexuality and anti-government riots. The vision can be regarded as a manifestation of these perils and of José's need to recognize and come to terms with his own instincts. Social and psychic order are menaced as chaotic forces threaten stability. This is also the chapter in which Rialta advises her son to accept the most difficult challenges but to pursue them in an intellectual rather than a physical realm.

The references that establish the context of José's vision are important, but there is an additional one that is perhaps even more crucial. Just before the scandal involving the athlete at the university, José had participated in a demonstration and received his mother's important advice upon his return home. He spends most of that night reading two books: Goethe's *Wilhelm Meister's Apprenticeship* and Gaius Suetonius Tranquillus's *The Lives of the Caesars*. Goethe's novel concerns a young man's aspirations to be a playwright and an actor, and José is so moved by a passage concerning the calm control of one's circumstance that he writes "¿Yo?" (249; "I?" 231) in the margin. Under the guidance of a mysterious society, Wilhelm's goals change. The society's influence on his movement toward maturity parallels to a certain extent Oppiano Licario's effect on José in the last chapters of *Paradiso*. José reads in Suetonius's book that Nero was particularly tormented in his last days by portents of impending disaster.[21] From Suetonius's portrayal José gains an appreciation of the tragic results of egocentric excesses. He applies his understanding of the meaning of the word *Neronic* to Foción in other sections of

21. George W. Mooney, in his introduction to Suetonius Tranquillus, *The Lives of the Caesars*, wrote: "One of the most striking features of the biographies is the importance attached by Suetonius to dreams and omens of every kind" (19).

Paradiso and seems to incorporate this vision of reality into his own artistic perception.

Within the context of these elements and episodes, José moves toward a commitment to writing and begins to react to readings and experiences by transforming the world he perceives. Chapter 12 can be regarded as the result of this dialectic between creativity and experience, and whether one considers the chapter as a compendium of dreams, visions, or writings, it is clear that they are intimately related to José Cemí. If the chapter consists of dreams, as Lezama Lima has stated, then José's life is an important source of the dreams' contents. This conclusion makes it possible to locate chapter 12 within rather than outside of the novel's plot and fabula. José's direct and indirect experiences, his conflicts, and, most importantly, his desires are manifested in the narrative process of chapter 12. In addition, his readings give him access to the memories of other times and places. Lezama Lima stated: "La memoria es un plasma del alma, es siempre creadora, espermática, pues memorizamos desde la raíz de la especie"[22] (A51).

In the same letter in which he indicated that chapter 12 is a collection of dreams, Lezama Lima wrote: "La novela es una vida, la de José Cemí, y la mía, que está metida por cada una de sus esquinas"[23] (A52). The importance of autobiographical elements in *Paradiso* will be considered in the next chapter of this study, but it is interesting to note here that Lezama Lima used the singular throughout the above references to encompass both his life and that of the character he created. It is as if a synthesis of identities had taken place in the author's mind. This recalls an earlier observation that there are indications that some of the characters in chapter 12 are fragmented. The merging and separation of identities that takes place is related to the consciousness through which the narration is filtered. The chapter evidences two tendencies that were present throughout Lezama Lima's career: the fragmentation of the authorial self into many entities and the avoidance of closure.

22. Lezama Lima, *La expresión americana* (Madrid: Alianza Editorial, 1969), 23.
23. Lezama Lima, *Cartas*, 94.

Whether the creator of chapter 12 is José Cemí, Lezama Lima, or, as Irlemar Chiampi Cortez has asserted, Oppiano Licario,[24] it is clear that the chapter emphasizes the transformations that take place in the process of writing, as well as the fact that the contents are closely related to José. A dedication to creative writing unites all of chapter 12's possible sources. But the focalization of the narration is predominantly through José; that is, it is through his eyes or consciousness that we enter this exceptional world of the imagination. In this regard, the central character in the novel participates in the creation and transformation of the text.

So many writers and characters have been submitted to the psychoanalyst's couch that one is hesitant to bring up the subject, but there are elements in the chapter that lend themselves well to this type of analysis. When the stroller looks into Juan Longo's coffin, he sees the child of chapter 12's second story. If the viewer and the child are regarded as aspects of the same person, it can be surmised that the stroller has emerged from childhood and come to terms with this element of his past and being. The child can be regarded as a figure that points simultaneously to the past and to the future. As a representative of the past, he suggests what has been overcome; and in reference to the future, he symbolizes the innocence of a new

24. Chiampi Cortez, "La proliferación barroca en *Paradiso.*" Chiampi Cortez refers to a sentence from *Las eras imaginarias* to justify her claim ("Oppiano Licario quiere provocar la sobrenaturaleza"), but it should be pointed out that Lezama Lima was referring here to the subject of time in the last three chapters of *Paradiso* and in the novel in general. When he speaks expressly of the narration of chapter 12, Lezama Lima uses the first-person singular: "Muevo la enormidad de un hacha, logro velocidades infinitas, veo los ciegos en los mercados nocturnos conversando sobre la calidad plástica de las fresas, al final, los soldados romanos, jugando a la Taba entre las ruinas, logro la tetractis, el cuatro, dios" (Lezama Lima, *Las eras imaginarias*, 182). Lezama Lima's comments indicate that a fragmentation of self-referential signs is taking place in chapter 12, and in this process the authorial self and some of the characters merge and separate. Eloísa Lezama Lima has commented on this synthesis of identities, particularly as it occurs in *Oppiano Licario:* "Lezama Lima no ha negado la transmigración de Licario, pero la mejor elucidación del personaje ocurre en la continuación de *Paradiso:* Licario será Fronesis buscando a su madre; Licario será Cemí; pero, en esencia, Licario será un inagotable recurso literario; será Lezama Lima y su afán de resurrección: 'no puede ser, no estoy muerto.' " (Eloísa Lezama Lima, "*Paradiso:* novela poema," 72). See also Emir Rodríguez Monegal, "*Paradiso* en su contexto," 42–43.

beginning and commitment. The meaning of Longo's wife seeing Flaminio in the casket is more complex, but the unmasking of glory (Flaminio's military past) can be related to death. Military uniforms are so often associated with José's concept of death in *Paradiso* that it is difficult to avoid the connection and its ultimate origin—the Colonel. There are so many vivid episodes in which the asthmatic José is overwhelmed by his father's dynamic presence, that one can speculate that the appearance of the uniformed Flaminio in the coffin represents José's moving out from under the shadow of his father—a necessary step in individual development.[25]

Chapter 12's assault on time represents an integration of the past (Atrio Flaminio, the grandmother, aspects of the child), the present (the stroller), and the future (the acceptance of life's flow into death, the commitment to art, and the child as innocence). This apprehension of temporal unity is also manifested in the simultaneous presence of memory (the past), intuition (the present), and desire or expectation (the future). The chapter contains stimulating allusions to José's former experiences, his present condition, and his desire to be a writer, and this unit of the novel suggests José's attainment of a sense of wholeness. When the four stories merge, the last line reads: "Ya el crítico percibe las gotas de lo temporal, pero no como el resto de los mortales, pues la muerte, no el sueño, comienza a regarle, ahora si de verdad, lo eterno, donde ya el tiempo no se deja vencer, ha comenzado por no existir ese pecado" (427; A53). The sin is the attempt to resist time's flow toward death, which is only a passage into the realm of the eternal. But sin and time are also synonymous, since they both contain the seeds of destruction. The only escape is passage into eternity. Chapter 12 contains the type of logic found in a dream, in that anything can happen and everything is possible. In this realm in which imagination is truly free, time and space hardly exist and memories and desires are synthesized.

Chapters 12 and 13 represent Lezama Lima's most ambitious efforts to escape the limitations of time and space, and these

25. An interesting approach to this possibility is found in Enrico Mario Santí, "Parridiso." See also footnote 8 in Chapter 6 of this study.

sections contain some of the most expansive parts of *Paradiso*. These chapters are so inventive that limiting elements are found mainly in subtle references to other sections of the text. Chapter 12 particularly questions the cohesion of the novel and challenges the reader's ability to uncover the networks of associations that Lezama Lima skillfully interweaved throughout his masterpiece. It reflects an inventive flight of the imagination as José initiates his commitment to creativity, and limiting elements are found in previous associations to his life. This transformation of the personal into creative art re-creates a relationship that exists between Lezama Lima and his fictional world, which is a process that is examined in the next chapter. To a certain extent, chapter 12 contains metaliterary elements in that it consists of a text that is generated within and from a work that relates how a young man becomes a writer. Within this process, a fragmentation of authorial identity takes place as aspects of Lezama Lima's life and being merge with different characters.

When considered within the context of its appearance, chapter 12 is functionally placed. It cannot be interpreted without recourse to other sections of *Paradiso*, and these relations of meaning contribute to the cohesion of the chapter and of the text as a whole. Like chapter 6, chapter 12 operates as a focal point of past and future events. Chapter 12 attempts to collapse time and is followed by a chapter that seeks to reduce the importance of space. Many characters who had previously only appeared in chapter 2 are encountered in chapter 13 as José moves toward the mysteries of art under the guidance of Oppiano Licario. Chapter 13 contains many elements that José must overcome in his movement toward manhood. The last two chapters (13 and 14) present his initiation into another stage of his life, and as the novel closes, José is ready to embark on a new, adventurous career.

Although length is clearly only one of many indicators of significance and not necessarily the most important, a survey of the relative length of the fourteen chapters that compose *Paradiso* (diagram C) discloses some interesting information. Half of the novel's fourteen chapters exceed twenty-five

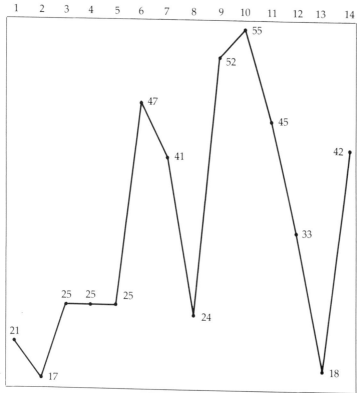

Diagram C

pages, and the other seven are twenty-five pages long or shorter. It is significant that the three longest chapters (9, 10, and 11) focus on José's university days and his friendships with Fronesis and Foción. A concern with peer relationships is predominant in these chapters. After chapter 11 Fronesis and Foción disappear; their absence is another sign that José has reached a new stage of development. It is interesting to note that the three longest chapters are followed by ones that attempt to collapse time and space (12, 13), and also that there is a parallel and rapid diminishing of length when this occurs. These chapters are followed by the last chapter (14), which is one of the longest. It is characterized by many archetypal events and by enigmatic language that thickens the prose and slows the reader's progress. The language challenges the reader to struggle with the signifying process of the text, just as José struggles through the darkness of the unknown: "Cemí siguió avanzando en la noche que se espesa, sintiendo que tenía que hacer cada vez más esfuerzo para penetrarla" (484; A54).

In many respects the thematic content is communicated by the physicality of the text. The novel closes with the words "podemos empezar" (489; "we can begin," 466). This ending that signifies a beginning suggests that a new plot and fabula are about to be set in motion as life's processes of dissolution and renewal continue. Since *Paradiso* is one of Lezama Lima's most autobiographical works, its conclusion is indicative of the importance of creativity in his life. The next chapter further examines this relationship between Lezama Lima's life and art, particularly as manifested in *Paradiso*.

5

The Autobiographical Paradox

Emir Rodríguez Monegal has described *Paradiso* as an "auto-biographical work."[1] Although it is a novel in the sense that it is a fictional narrative, *Paradiso* is also, to a degree, autobiographical, in that it constitutes a search for origins in family history, creates a self-portrait, and uses the author's life as a referent. There are numerous correspondences between Lezama Lima's personal and professional life and *Paradiso*.[2] Among the most striking is the use of his parents, José María Lezama y Rodda and Rosa María Lima y Rosaldo, as models for the Colonel and Rialta. The death of Lezama Lima's father, an artillery colonel in the Cuban army, left the same emptiness in the family's life as it does in the novel. And the author's struggle against asthma, an illness that first appeared when he was less than a year old and plagued him the rest of his life, also marks the existence of José Cemí. After the death of his father, Lezama Lima's mother suggested that he become the family's historian, a charge that he successfully carried out with the creation of his masterpiece. However, whether or not *Paradiso* can be classified as an autobiography depends to a great extent on one's definition of this literary form.

The concept of autobiography has been undergoing radical change in recent critical theory. William L. Howarth has pointed out that "for too long critics have held that autobiography is 'unique,' that is, unprecedented but also monolithic in

1. Rodríguez Monegal, *The Borzoi Anthology of Latin American Literature*, 2:629.

2. For an informative description of the autobiographical elements in *Paradiso*, see Eloísa Lezama Lima, "Mi hermano." See also José Lezama Lima, "Confluencias," in *Las eras imaginarias*, 171–93. The latter work was also published as "Autoretrato poético," in his *Cangrejos y golondrinas*, 9–32. A literary treatment of Lezama Lima's professional life is contained in Lorenzo García Vega, *Los años de orígenes*. Also very useful is Cintio Vitier's introductory essay to Lezama Lima, *Obras completas* 1:11–64.

form. I hope to encourage a new response, one that finds more variety among the works and more similarity to established literary genres. If we can see that autobiographers do not always share the same principles, then we should no longer have to read them with a single set of values."[3] Recent research indicates that a more open concept of autobiography is beginning to prevail as scholars turn their attention to the autobiographical implications of works as diverse as Soren Kierkegaard's *Repetition* and Sigmund Freud's *Interpretation of Dreams*.[4] This trend toward a more open definition has been accompanied by serious questioning of the notions of author, the self, and writing.[5] William C. Spengemann, in his study of the evolution of autobiography from St. Augustine to Nathaniel Hawthorne, classifies works under the headings of historical, philosophical, or poetic autobiography. According to Spengemann, Hawthorne's *Scarlet Letter* dismisses the assumption that a substantial self or soul precedes and governs individual experience and may be discerned through that experience. This assumption had enabled historical autobiographers to explain, philosophical autobiographers to search for, and poetic autobiographers to express, the absolute self behind their conditioned actions. Those autobiographers who have managed to maintain Augustine's belief in uncon-

3. Howarth, "Some Principles of Autobiography," in *Autobiography*, ed. James Olney, 88. An extensive bibliographical survey of the study of autobiography is contained in William C. Spengemann, *The Forms of Autobiography*, 170–245.

4. Michael Sprinkler, "Fictions of the Self: The End of Autobiography," in *Autobiography*, ed. James Olney, 321–42. Sprinkler refers to *Repetition* as "a searching critique of the similarities and differences between recollection and repetition, couched in the form that Freud was to make famous—the case history" (Ibid., 329), and to *The Interpretation of Dreams* as "an autobiography and the foundation of all of Freud's theoretical writing" (Ibid., 337). For a structuralist interpretation of autobiography, which is based in part on the texts of Sigmund Freud and Jacques Lacan, see Jeffrey Mehlman, *A Structural Study of Autobiography*. Mehlman states: "For Freud was, I believe, the practitioner of the most radical form of autobiography we know: that self-analysis which, beginning in the correspondence with Fliess, was pursued throughout his career and, no doubt, in and through his most difficult 'theoretical' works" (Ibid., 14).

5. See particularly Sprinkler, "Fictions of the Self"; and Louis A. Renza, "The Veto of the Imagination: A Theory of Autobiography," in *Autobiography*, ed. James Olney, 268–95.

ditioned selfhood have continued to write about themselves in the three forms he erected upon that belief. But, for those who have accepted Hawthorne's conclusion, that the self is continually reshaped by efforts to explain, discover, or express it, autobiography in the Augustinian sense is no longer possible."[6] Spengemann concludes that the modern concept of autobiography makes "autobiography seem both impossible and unavoidable. Without a self, one cannot write about it, but whatever one writes will be about the self it constructs. Autobiography thus becomes synonymous with symbolic action in any form, and the word ceases to designate a particular kind of writing. To call any modernist work 'autobiographical' is merely to utter a tautology."[7]

Whether or not one unreservedly accepts this contemporary view of autobiography, it does contain implications that are germane to our consideration of *Paradiso*. Lezama Lima's statement that he was and was not José Cemí indicates that he recognized the paradoxical role that autobiography plays in his masterpiece.[8] The recognition of this dialectic is central to any consideration of the narrative strategy in *Paradiso*, because there are instances in the text in which the distinction between the self as narrator and the self as object of the narration is evident. Howarth has referred to these two functions as "the persona's two didactic roles: as narrator, he teaches his prime lesson; as protagonist he relives and learns from his days of sin or error."[9] This dichotomy is evident in the passage that describes José seeing the wax figure of a saint and confusing it with death. José and his grandmother are first referred to as Doña Augusta and "her grandson," but these identities suddenly change to "my grandmother" and "I." "Al pasar delante de la urna que reproduce en cera a Santa Flora muerta, Doña Augusta le dijo a su nieto: —Es una santica que está ahí, muerta de verdad—. La cera de la cara y de las manos perfeccionaba lo que yo, por indicación de mi Abuela y por descono-

---

6. Spengemann, *The Forms of Autobiography*, 167.
7. Ibid., 168.
8. "Aun el mismo José Cemí es y no es mi persona" (Lezama Lima, *Cartas*, 22).
9. Howarth, "Some Principles of Autobiography," 9.

cimiento de que existiesen esos trabajos en cera, creía que era la verdadera muerte"[10] (A55). The narration then returns to the third person and points out that at the age of six, José could scarcely make the necessary distinctions. Such dramatic shifts in the narration underscore the autobiographical element in the novel and are indicative of the juxtaposition of two time frames: the time of the event and that of the observation that José could not understand the situation because of his youth.

There are many examples of these narrative shifts and time juxtapositions throughout the text. The most dramatic is the observation made immediately after José's mother advises him to always attempt the most difficult. She closes her advisory discourse with reference to a future that may deny that her counsel was ever given. "Algunos impostores pensarán que yo nunca dije estas palabras, que tú las has invencionado, pero cuando tú des la respuesta por el testimonio, tú y yo sabremos que sí las dije mientras viva y que tú las seguirás diciendo después que me haya muerto" (246; A56). At this point, in what seems to be an attempt to carry out Rialta's prediction, the narrator states in the first person: "Sé que esas son las palabras más hermosas que Cemí oyó en su vida, después de las que leyó en los evangelios, y que nunca oirá otras que lo pongan tan decisivamente en marcha, pero fueron tantas las cosas que recayeron en ese día sobre él, que comenzó a sentir esa indecisión nerviosa que precede a la sibilación bronquial de una crisis asmática" (246; A57). Here the narrator's identification with José becomes complete, and a synthesis of the present ("sé"), past ("oyó"), and future ("oirá") is conveyed by the verbal forms that are used. The narrator interrupts a scene that is in progress and relates information that could only be known after a lapse of time. In this regard, the temporal context of the narrator and that of José and his mother are quite different, and therefore the flow of the action is momentarily suspended by the narrator's presence. Although the reader is partially prepared for this interruption by the time displacements that are conveyed by the verbal sequences in Rialta's

10. Lezama Lima, *Paradiso* (Mexico City: Ediciones Era, 1968), 153. Subsequent quotations are from this edition and are noted in the text.

speech and by the presentation of her discourse in the first-person singular, the narrator's comments are surprising.

It is clear from such examples that Lezama Lima's self-referential sign in *Paradiso* is not only *I* but also *José Cemí*. One can surmise that the *I* functions as a sign of autobiographical intentionality, and that in the previously cited narrative shifts, fictional and autobiographical intentionality confront one another. Rialta's fears that her advice will be considered a fiction seem to echo the narrator's concern that the distinctions between autobiography and fiction will be lost. Verifiability becomes a crucial concern in Rialta's and the narrator's observations, and, to answer this issue, the narrator breaks in and verifies the truth of the matter by using the first-person singular in the present tense. This is a curious technique, for the narrator becomes his own referent and substantiates his own sources; that is, he signifies the importance of these events in his life by insisting on their verifiability.

In this instance of confrontation between autobiographical and fictional modes, the self becomes an object and contemplates itself; or the self, in an attempt to resist its own objectivization in the text, asserts its presence in order to avoid the alienation that writing entails. When the *I* breaks into the text, superimposing its mark on José, a synthesis of identities and times is attempted. One can speculate that these intrusions are indicative not only of the issue of verifiability but also of an anxiety about the loss of the self that is involved in writing. As Michael Sprinkler has stated: "No autobiography can take place except within the boundaries of a writing where concepts of subject, self, and author collapse into the act of producing a text."[11] There is also a confrontation with the barriers of time and space, since autobiographical elements are linked to memory. James Olney points out: "In the act of remembering the past in the present, the autobiographer imagines into existence another person, another world, and surely it is *not* the same, in any real sense, as that past world that does not, under any

---

11. Sprinkler, "Fictions of the Self," 342. It is interesting to note that there is only one footnote in *Paradiso*, in which it is stated: "Es más natural el artificio del arte fictivo, como es más artificial lo natural nacido sustituyendo" (452).

circumstances, nor however much we may wish it, now exist."[12]

In Lezama Lima's creative world, these dilemmas are often couched in terms of absence and distance, as in the following examples concerning José. "Otra frase que tenía como un relieve druídico, la más intocable lejanía familiar, donde los rostros se desvanecían como si los viésemos por debajo del mar . . . era esa palabra de *oidor*, oída y saboreada por José Cemí como la clave imposible de un mundo desconocido" (50; A58). In this case the word *hearer*, or *judge*, becomes an indicator of the simultaneous presence and absence of an unrecoverable past, of a trace that embodies absence. And in the following quotation, José becomes a sign of the dialectic between the past and the present, particularly as they are related to his dead father. "Esa visibilidad de la ausencia, ese dominio de la ausencia, era el más fuerte signo de Cemí. En él lo que no estaba, estaba; lo invisible ocupaba el primer plano en lo visible, convirtiéndose en un visible de una vertiginosa posibilidad; la ausencia era presencia, penetración" (349; A59). The designation of absence as José's sign indirectly touches on the paradoxical aspect of the dialectic between autobiographical and fictional modes. The sign refers simultaneously to the embodiment of absence and to memory's desire to overcome the barriers of time and space in order to recapture the past. This quotation is followed by a summary of José's family tree, which represents the self's inquiry into its own history, and then the narrative proceeds to a contemplation of creativity. In this and many other sections of the novel, the primary purpose of the language is aesthetic, while the goal of the content is self-understanding.

Although *Paradiso* gained immediate critical acclaim, it also received a gread deal of notoriety because of its frank and explicit exploration of sexuality in general and of homosexuality in particular. The first edition, which was published in Cuba, was small by Cuban standards—only four thousand copies—and, as far as I know, a second edition has never appeared in that country.[13] Lezama Lima seems to have been

12. Olney, "The Ontology of Autobiography," in his *Autobiography*, 241.
13. For a discussion of this topic, see Emir Rodríguez Monegal, "La nueva

puzzled by the notoriety. In a letter written in 1974, he mentioned resistance to the publication of *Paradiso* in Spain and stated that he could not understand how this could have occurred, since Mario Vargas Llosa's *Pantaleón y las visitadoras* had been published there.[14] It is true that there is a far greater emphasis on sexuality in Vargas Llosa's novel, but the humorous escapades of that work deal only with heterosexual relations, and the novel's treatment of the subject is not as broad or comprehensive as *Paradiso's* exploration of this complex aspect of human conduct. The initial resistance to *Paradiso* was most likely related to homosexuality, which is a particularly sensitive subject in Hispanic society. *Paradiso* was eventually published in Spain.

As in most cases of this sort, the sexual content of *Paradiso* has frequently been overemphasized or misinterpreted.[15] Within the content of the novel, sexuality is presented as merely a part of existence and as one that offers as many dangers as pleasures. The only advocate of homosexuality is the bisexual Foción, and he is presented as a tormented soul who suffers a mental breakdown. José's other close friend, Fronesis, overcomes his inability to perform with a girlfriend, and form is successfully imposed upon psychic disorder. Indeed, sexuality is presented as a force that must be controlled if it is not to overwhelm and destroy individuals.

Although *Paradiso* explores a variety of sexual conduct and considers some of the philosophical justifications for different patterns of behavior, it does not constitute an affirmation of any particular sexual code. Rather, sexuality is presented as

novela vista desde Cuba." Lorenzo García Vega also discusses the publication of *Paradiso* as well as Lezama Lima's attitudes toward the novel's sexual contents in his *Los años de orígenes*, 69.

14. "Ahí se ha publicado *Pantaleón y las visitadoras*, que tiene muchas más cosas de intimidad sexual que las que conlleva toda mi novela. Y en una forma más descarnada y realista" (Lezama Lima, *Cartas*, 259).

15. For intelligent discussions of the subject of homosexuality in *Paradiso*, see Enrique Lihn, "*Paradiso*, novela y homosexualidad"; and Emir Rodríguez Monegal, "*Paradiso* en su contexto." Lihn makes the following astute observations: "Creo necesario el reconocimiento de que el *discurso valorativo* de *Paradiso* (el cual no agota en absoluto la novela) y *la historia* (el destino de Foción entre otros) condena y castiga a la homosexualidad, intentan quizá exorcizarla, le contra-ponen 'una categoría superior al sexo,' la androginia perfecta y creadora de Cemí" (Lihn, "*Paradiso*," 16–17).

one of many possible dangers on the road to salvation and as a force that, when misused, can become a narcissistic whirlpool of self-destruction. Rodríguez Monegal has pointed out that Lezama Lima's creative system:

> tiene en su centro la noción de salvación y que encuentra como vía para la salvación la creación poética. Quienes olvidan que Lezama es católico, olvidan que es un poeta católico y que sólo en tanto que tal es posible comprender hondamente su sistema. De ahí que la novela se llama *Paradiso*, y no sólo como superficial homenaje al otro gran poeta católico. El hombre de Lezama, desterrado del paraíso de la infancia, perdido en el mundo, se salva por la poesía. Contra la afirmación heidergeriana de que el hombre es para la muerte, alza Lezama su profunda convicción de que el hombre es para la resurrección y de que esa resurrección llega por el camino de la poesía.[16] (A60)

This system that views creative writing as a way to salvation contains its own dangers. Metaliterature, autobiography, and excessive sexuality all contain self-referential elements, which, paradoxically, can lead either to narcissistic self-indulgence or to self-knowledge. Exploring the demarcation between the two can be a dangerous enterprise.

Eloísa Lezama Lima has pointed out that her brother would often synthesize the characteristics of three undistinguished relatives into one colorful character.[17] Given this aspect of Lezama Lima's creative process, it is unwise to attempt to establish one-to-one relationships between fictive and "real" individuals. One can assume that the process worked in a reverse fashion in the autobiographical mode—that the authorial self was fragmented and projected onto numerous characters. In *Paradiso* this occurs particularly in regard to sexuality. With the exception of a brief encounter on a Florida beach with Grace Ginsley, an "older" woman of sixteen years, José does not participate directly in any sexual activity. But codes that refer to sexuality are embedded in many passages. In *Paradiso* Lezama Lima obviously chose to displace this aspect of his autobiography, so that his sexual life and the sexual lives of his immediate family would be decorously concealed. The ab-

16. Rodríguez Monegal, "*Paradiso* en su contexto," *Imagen*, 5.
17. Lezama Lima, *Cartas*, 22.

sence of much overt sexualty in the case of José might be indicative of what the author would have liked to have been, at least in a theological sense. This is particularly significant as far as the autobiographical mode is concerned, for it represents a departure from the model used in *Paradiso*. The narrative strategy is different in his second novel, *Oppiano Licario*, which was published posthumously and incomplete in 1977. In this work, which is in many respects a satellite of *Paradiso*, José sleeps with the title character's sister.

When asked if he considered *Paradiso* an autobiographical work, Lezama Lima replied that the novel responded to a particular circumstance—that of the family—and moved to the abstract realm of archetypes and mythology.[18] This procedure explains the novel's movement from the specific to the general and reflects Lezama Lima's concern in capturing universal essences. He places José within a specific family in a particular social class, relates the family to a national cultural heritage, and then moves to a universal cultural context by referring to numerous mythologies. This explains, in part, the abstract nature of the last chapters of the novel and the obscurity of some passages in which several cultural ideologies are synthesized.

According to Thomas E. Lewis, the literary referent is a "cultural ideological unit" that is encoded into a text, and it communicates a semantic field throughout the work.[19] Wolfgang Iser includes such cultural contexts in what he terms the "repertoire," which he defines as consisting "of all the familiar territory within the text. This may be in the form of references to earlier works, or to social and historical norms, or to the whole culture from which the text has emerged."[20]

On one level, Lezama Lima defines what it means to be Cuban, and on a more philosophical and theological plane, he relates José to conditions found in all times and places. José Juan Arrom, who has delineated many of the Cuban elements

18. "Interrogando a Lezama Lima," in *Recopilación de textos sobre José Lezama Lima*, ed. Pedro Simón Martínez, 21.
19. Lewis, "Notes toward a Theory of the Referent," 463.
20. Iser, *The Act of Reading*, 69. I have also been helped a great deal by John S. Brushwood, "Sobre el referente y la transformación narrativa."

that can be found in *Paradiso*, has pointed out that *cemí* is a word of Tainian origin. The Tainos tribe was the largest of numerous Indian tribes that occupied Cuba before the arrival of the Spanish, and, Arrom explains, they used the word *cemí* to designate the gods and the images that represented them.[21] Arrom is undoubtedly correct, for Lezama Lima has said that at the end of the novel José moves to "complementar su patronímico de ídolo o imagen" (complement his surname as idol or image).[22] Taking this line of association a step further, an explanation by Fernando Ortiz that "taíño" indicates a social category associated with nobility and dominion should be noted. According to Ortiz, the Tainians represented the most advanced culture in pre-Hispanic Cuba.[23] Within the world of *Paradiso*, the Cemí family enjoys these social attributes or distinctions.

Arrom also claims that the title of the book is not based on Dante but is instead based on a reference in a poetic myth to Cuba—the paradise of the Tainos.[24] This poeticization of legend or myth is alluded to by Lezama Lima in his comments on the appearance of Oppiano Licario's sister in the closing chapters. "Aparece la hermana Inaca Eco Licario rindiendo la sentencia poética como la tierra prometida"[25] (A61). The vision of a promised land is part of a national tradition. This relationship and Lezama Lima's understanding of it are discussed in Cintio Vitier's *Lo cubano en la poesía*.[26] Lezama Lima belonged to a generation that was obsessed with defining what it means to be Cuban, and his concept of Cuban culture was influenced by other thinkers, particularly Fernando Ortiz. *Paradiso* is indebted in both a general and a specific sense to Fernando Ortiz. This indebtedness is evidenced in the recognition of the

21. Arrom, "Lo tradicional cubano en el mundo novelístico de José Lezama Lima," 470. See also Arrom, *Mitología y artes prehispánicas en las Antillas*; and Fernando Ortiz, *Contrapunto cubano del tabaco y el azúcar*, particularly part 2, chapter 6.

22. Lezama Lima, *Las eras imaginarias*, 183.

23. Ortiz, *Los factores humanos de la cubanidad*, 18.

24. Arrom, "Lo tradicional cubano en el mundo novelístico de José Lezama Lima," 470.

25. Lezama Lima, *Las eras imaginarias*, 183.

26. Vitier, *Lo cubano en la poesía*. See particularly chapters 1 and 13. See also his introductory essay to Lezama Lima, *Obras completas*.

tobacco and sugar industries' influence on the formation of Cuban character and in the understanding that the pre-Hispanic ritual of smoking is part of the cultural code in contemporary Cuba and communicates opulence and dominance. These few examples of the many manifestations of Cuban cultural tradition in *Paradiso* are indicative of the work's preoccupation with an apprehension of Cuban essence. The novel recognizes pre-Hispanic Indian civilizations as a central component of Cuban identity and reflects the successive incorporations of European, black, and oriental cultures. There are also allusions in the novel to the influence of the Indian civilizations of the American continent, particularly in the section concerning the Colonel's trip to Mexico. References to the United States include the Colonel's military training in Florida, his death in Florida during the great influenza epidemic of 1918–1919, and Rialta's family's residence in the same state in an earlier time. All of these episodes closely parallel the history of Lezama Lima's family.

This preoccupation with cultural tradition is particularly prevalent in the novel because of that genre's historic connection with Cuban national identity. The development of the novel in Spanish America coincided with the independence movement of the nineteenth century. (During the colonial period, which lasted three hundred years, there was a curious absence of what contemporary critics would define as novels.) The novel was intimately related to the development of a national identity, because, of all the verbal art forms, it most fully engages a wide range of cultural communications. In *Paradiso* the interest in the development of a national consciousness is manifested in references to some of the forces that shaped Cuban personality: Cuba's pre-Hispanic heritage, its geographical setting, its history, and its two major sources of economic vitality—tobacco and sugar.

Lezama Lima also incorporates into his repertoire a number of other cultural ideological units. Philosophical, literary, musical, and mythological references abound throughout the work. A representative sampling of the mythological references includes Angra Mainyu (101; 91), the Persian personification of darkness and evil; Osiris (270; 252), the Egyptian god of the underworld; Siva (106; 97), in Hindu myth the third deity in the triad of great gods; Semiramis (232; 215), the legendary queen of Assyria; Moloch (229; 213), the sun-god of the Ammonites; Ananke (423; 400), a Greek goddess who personified fate; Terminus (259; 241), the Roman god of boundaries; the Valkyries (296; 276), in Norse myth the maidens of the supreme deity; Xibalbá (42; 36), the realm of evil in Mayan mythology; and Viracocha (378; 357), the supreme deity of the ancient Peruvians.[27] Mythologies are systems of images that explain or interpret the world, and myths are the themes of the imagination. These systems communicate humankind's awe at the mysteries of life, explain the universe by giving it form, support and validate different social orders, and help guide the individual through the crises of life.[28] Although the mythologies are varied and belong to different times and places, they communicate essential messages that continually repeat themselves, and they are based on experiences that are universal. In *Paradiso* José Cemí discovers a particular social order and the world, passes through the threshold that separates childhood from adulthood, and embarks on an adventurous quest—the commitment to creativity. He moves from the security of formal social and family structures to the insecurity of the new and creative. The many mythological references in *Paradiso* indicate that José is not only an extension of Cuban qualities; he is also a child of the world, because he embodies essences and experiences that belong to all of us. Lezama Lima's frequent use of archetypal and mythological figures also recalls Spengemann's observation that, since Hawthorne, a modern concept of autobiography is synonymous with symbolic action.

In considering how the major extratextual realities function in the novel and how they are transformed into narrative, it is helpful to consider Gérard Genette's concept of the expansion of a verb—an idea he suggests in his introduction to an analysis of a work by Proust. "Since any narrative, even one as

27. Frank Chapin Bray, *Bray's University Dictionary of Mythology*; Joseph Kaster, *Putnam's Concise Mythological Dictionary*; Felix Guirand, ed., *New Larousse Encyclopedia of Mythology*.
28. Joseph Campbell, *The Masks of God*, 608–24.

extensive and complex as the *Recherche du temps perdu*, is a linguistic production undertaking to tell one of several events, it is perhaps legitimate to treat it as the development—monstrous, if you will—given to a *verbal* form, in the grammatical sense of the term: the expansion of a verb. *I walk, Pierre has come* are for me minimal forms of narrative, and inversely the *Odyssey* or the *Recherche* is only, in a certain way, an amplification (in the rhetorical sense) of statements such as *Ulysses comes home to Ithaca* or *Marcel becomes a writer.*"[29]

If we apply Genette's concept to *Paradiso*, the following scheme emerges: (1) the autobiographical paradox (I am/am not José Cemí), (2) Cuba (José Cemí is Cuban), (3) other cultures (José Cemí discovers the world), and (4) creativity (José Cemí becomes a writer). A process of definition and discovery underlies these four categories. The first involves the self's inquiry into its own being; the second, a contemplation of what it means to be Cuban; the third, the revelation of an individual's connection to universal human experience as symbolized in culture; and the fourth, the dialectical relationship that exists between creativity and the first three categories. The last point is particularly important, for as José becomes committed to writing, he transforms extratextual realities.

These categories contain the paradoxical processes of closure and aperture, in the sense that they synthesize a self-contemplative stance and an openness to all that is exterior. This contradiction enhances many of the novel's concerns, for if any one characteristic can be said to be lurking in the shadows of Lezama Lima's creative world, it is a thirst for absolutes. And absolutes can only be discovered in a relentless investigation of the self and the world. For this reason Lezama Lima once referred to Oppiano Licario, who shows José the way to creativity, as a "new Icarus who was trying to attempt the impossible."[30]

The four categories begin as extratextual realities, but as they are encoded into the text, they become semantic fields that are

29. Gérard Genette, *Narrative Discourse*, 30.
30. Lezama Lima, *Las eras imaginarias*, 182.

interwoven throughout the novel. Each one, individually or in combination with others, tends to predominate in certain sections of the text. Generally speaking, the first two prevail in the first chapters of *Paradiso*, and the third and fourth are predominant in the concluding sections of the work. The novel moves from the first to the last categories; it is a work in which the specifics of an autobiographical context are transformed and moved into a creative apprehension of the world. The chapter that operates as a prototype of this process is chapter 12, in which José fictionalizes elements from his life and projects them into the realm of myth. However, chapter 12 cannot stand alone, because its significance is lost if it is isolated from the rest of the text. The message it conveys—the artistic transformation of certain contexts—is a central component of the novel.

Both an autobiographical and a fictive intentionality are indispensable to *Paradiso*; for this reason I have termed this process the autobiographical paradox. The work can be classified as an autobiographical novel or a fictionalized autobiography. Both terms reflect, with different degrees of emphasis, the mixture of autobiographical and fictive intentionality in *Paradiso*. Of the two terms, I prefer the second, because in my view it more accurately reflects the precise nature of the synthesis.

In an epistemological sense, the novel is a combination of autobiography and fiction. On a stylistic level, the novel represents a blending of narrative prose and poetry. On an ideological level, it represents a mixture of anarchistic and conservative tendencies. It is conservative in its emphasis on family and social values and anarchistic in certain instances in regard to an insistence on immediate sexual gratification. The novel affirms some of the values that sustain the social order and challenges others. These syntheses are indicative of one of the major strategies of Lezama Lima's art: his attempt to integrate diverse and often contradictory elements. These contradictory modes have their origin in Lezama Lima's personal life, but some of these elements are displaced or projected onto characters other than José.

The repeated appearance of circle imagery in *Paradiso*, which has been referred to several times, is undoubtedly an important aspect of the novel. Cirlot points out that the circle can "stand for heaven and perfection and sometimes eternity as well," and that the Chinese symbol for heaven was a circle.[31] Lezama Lima also had recourse to a myth from India that associates the circle with the entrance to paradise. In one of his essays, he describes a river that ends in a seething circle of water that leads to paradise.[32]

The circle can also be applied to a conceptualization of the self, particularly as defined by Carl Jung, who saw the self as the "totality of the psyche. The self is not only the centre, but also the whole circumference which embraces both conscious and unconscious, it is the centre of this totality, just as the ego is the centre of consciousness."[33] This synthesis of symbolism, which deals with concepts of the exterior world and of the self, provides an important artistic linkage of two of the referents— autobiography and world culture. Geometric progressions from square to circle often appear in the novel. This occurs for a number of reasons, but particularly to convey the movement from potentiality to creativity. In this respect, circular imagery can be regarded as an artistic strategy that is used to unify the four referents. The first and fourth categories, autobiography and creativity, form the initial and final links of a circular creative process; they are the basis of a narration that continually contemplates itself even as it incorporates the external world into its own orbit. In this regard, the text presents the self's inquiry into its own history, its immersion into Cuban and other cultures, and its discovery and commitment to creativity.

The last chapter of *Paradiso* offers a masterful synthesis of the four major referents; they are subtly interwoven into a lush narrative fabric. Chapter 14 abounds in mythological and cultural allusions of national and international origins—it even

31. Juan Eduardo Cirlot, *A Dictionary of Symbols*, 45.
32. Lezama Lima, *Las eras imaginarias*, 192–93.
33. Jung, "Dream Symbolism in Relation to Alchemy," in *The Portable Jung*, 324.

contains references to Van Gogh's self-portraits. The chapter presents José's movement toward his commitment to poetry and Oppiano Licario's role in this event. It has two major divisions. The first, which is narrated with a great deal of wit and humor, concerns Licario's life, including his adventures in Europe. The second narrates José's metaphorical journey through a night of perils and possibilities. Lezama Lima has explained that José's nocturnal meanderings contain elements of exile and wanderings in the wilderness—a sense of separation and longing—and he has compared José's state to the feelings that he believes Cuba's national hero José Martí must have felt when he was released from prison in Spain.

> Después de su prisión, Martí debió de sentir como un renacer en la imagen de la resurrección, como después de su muerte vuelve a resurgir en la carne. Lo desértico y su nueva aparición simbólica en el destierro se igualan, y por eso en el *Paradiso*, para propiciar el último encuentro de José Cemí con Oppiano Licario, para llegar a la nueva casualidad, a la ciudad tibetana, tiene que atravesar todas las ocurrencias y recurrencias de la noche. El descendimiento placentario de lo nocturno, el fiel de la medianoche, aparecen como una variante del desierto y del destierro, todas las posibilidades del sistema poético han sido puestas en marcha, para que Cemí concurra a la cita con Licario.[34] (A62)

This skillful blending of the concepts of sacrifice, purification, death, resurrection, and creativity projects cultural elements into the realm of the eternal. For Lezama Lima, the poetic image represented a glimpse of eternity, because it entails a movement toward unity and represents a way of unifying the many fragments of existence. Imagery is a way of understanding the world, of relating visible reality to an order of existence beyond the observable universe.

During his nocturnal stroll, José sees a mosaic that depicts the Holy Grail in the center of a circle formed by King Arthur's knights. A manifestation of the circle image, the quest for the Grail represents the search for the mystic center—the nucleus of all being. José's passages into the mysteries of creativity represents the beginning of his search for paradise, and the

34. Lezama Lima, *Las eras imaginarias*, 182.

streets he wanders through are symbolic of the rivers that lead
to paradise. Separated for all time from the security of childhood, and unaccompanied by his friends, José confronts the
significance of Licario's demise and the void that death represents. Licario's wake provokes a chain of metonymic associations linked to death:

> Recordó el relato de doña Augusta, su bisabuelo muerto, con
> uniforme de gala, intacto, que de pronto, como un remolino
> invisible, se deshacía en un polvo coloreado. La cera de la cara y
> las manos, con su urna de cristal, de Santa Flora, ofreciendo una
> muerte resistente, dura como la imagen del cuerpo evaporado.
> La cera repentinamente propicia al trineo del tacto, ofreciendo
> un infinito deslizamiento. De nuevo la voz de su padre, escondi-
> do detrás de una columna, y diciéndole con voz fingida: —cuan-
> do nosotros estábamos vivos, andábamos por un camino, y
> ahora que estamos muertos, andamos por este otro—. Cobró
> vivencia de la frase "andar por el otro camino". Ascendió la
> imagen de Oppiano Licario, pero ya solo en el omnibus, con
> todos los demás asientos vacíos, sonando sus colecciones de
> medallas, mandando a detener al caballito de sus dracmas
> griegos, con sus pechos y sus ancas desproporcionados en rela-
> ción con la cara y con las patas pequeñas que rotaban sobre un
> tambor. El inmenso tambor de la noche, un tambor silencioso,
> que fabricaba ausencias, huecos, retiramientos, desconchados
> por los que cabía un brazo de mar. (488; A63)

The overwhelming emptiness that José feels at this moment is
skillfully conveyed by references to the unfathomable depths
of the sea and the "immense drum of the night." The allusions
to space, darkness, and the silence of the drum suggest the
sense of loss, chaos, and emotional disorientation that José
experiences on learning of Licario's death.

José is met by Licario's sister, and her self-assured manner,
which is partially conveyed by geometric forms, reassures
him. "Mostraba como su hermano una total confianza religiosa
en sí misma y ese sí mismo estaba formado por dos líneas que
se interceptaban en un punto. Y ese punto era el encuentro
entre su azar y su destino" (488; A64). The reference to fate and
destiny can also be applied to José and is soon repeated in lines
from a poem that Licario wrote for José. When José looks into
the coffin, which is sealed with a glass pane, the reader recalls

the Roman consul and the music critic in chapter 12. Atrio Flaminio's heroic feats and Juan Longo's attempts to negate time are now transferred to Licario, but, in a spiritual sense, he succeeds where they had failed. The glass pane is described as a "magic mirror," and it reflects light like a brilliant "radiation of ideas." "Como un espejo mágico captaba la radiación de las ideas, la columna de autodestrucción del conocimiento se levantaba con la esbeltez de la llama, se reflejaba en el espejo y dejaba su inscripción. Era la cola de Juno, el cielo estrellado que se reflejaba en el paréntesis de las constelaciones" (488–89; A65). The mention of Juno associates Licario with heroic deeds as well as with the forces of destiny, because, according to Lezama Lima, it is "the comet that announced the death of Julius Caesar."[35] This association recalls Rialta's admonition to José that the dangerous and the difficult can be encountered in intellectual as well as physical realms.

Oppiano Licario's sister, Ynaca Eco Licario, hands José her brother's poem, which is entitled "José Cemí." As he reads the work, he and the reader encounter the same text.

> No lo llamo, porque él viene,
> como dos astros cruzados
> en sus leyes encaramados
> 4 La órbita elíptica tiene.
>
> Yo estuve, pero él estará,
> cuando yo sea el puro conocimiento,
> la piedra traída en el viento,
> 8 en el egipcio paño de lino me envolverá.
>
> La razón y la memoria al alzar
> verán a la paloma alcanzar
> 11 La fe en la sobrenaturaleza.
>
> La araña y la imagen por el cuerpo,
> 13 no puede ser, no estoy muerto.
>
> 14 Vi morir a tu padre; ahora, Cemí, tropieza. (489; A66)

The first stanza is an affirmation of faith in destiny and the laws of the cosmos. Just as two stars can cross because of the elliptical orbits of their paths, Licario knew that this encounter between José and his text would take place. The second stanza continues this affirmation along with a synthesis of the past and the future as related to space. Licario predicts that when he is stone—pure being moving in the wind—and freed from materiality or simply a memory of what once existed, José will continue the traditions of the past. This act of preservation and memory is carried out by the inclusion of the poem in the text we read. This linkage of José to tradition is continued in line nine with the reference to memory, and Licario foretells José's movement toward a belief in a realm beyond the physical universe.

The twelfth line contains one of Lezama Lima's favorite images, the spider, which here suggests imagination, the self, and the circle. The spider's creative force is suggested by the web it weaves, and the concentric circles of its net move toward a central point. It is stated that the body cannot take the place of the spider and the image (I have in mind here the syntax caused by the rhyme scheme and the matching of verbs and subjects)—a suggestion that being and identity are not centered in the flesh. This sentiment is immediately followed in line thirteen by a denial of death (Cirlot states that thirteen is "symbolic of death and birth, a beginning afresh"[36]). This negation of death reinforces the imagery of the ninth line, in that both reflect Lezama Lima's belief that the impossible is believable simply because it is beyond the bounds of possibility or reason.[37] The poem attempts to convert time-bound elements into ones that are time-free, and it invites José to consider a limitation (death) as a door to possibility (imagination and eternity). Through his poetic composition Licario challenges José to see beyond the realm of limitations in which he lives in order to discover indications of infinite aperture. The poem closes with a reference to the death of the Colonel and with the suggestion that José is now ready to embark on his own sacrificial journey.

The poem has a profound influence on José and provokes a vision of the contending forces operating in existence and of the organization and unity that underlie the seeming chaos of

36. Cirlot, *Dictionary of Symbols*, 224.
37. Armando Alvarez Bravo, ed., *Orbita de Lezama Lima*, 40.

the world. José leaves the wake and goes to a coffee stand. As he stirs his coffee, the sound of the metal hitting the glass recalls Licario's words during an earlier ritualistic episode, and José recalls Licario's previous pronouncement that he is ready for a commitment to creativity. The novel terminates with the echo of Licario's words ringing in his mind: "Volvía a oir de nuevo: ritmo hesicástico, podemos empezar" (490; A67). The reference to the "rhythm of hesychasts" indicates that José has made it through a tumultuous passage and is ready for a period of contemplation.

A slight but significant modification of Licario's words has taken place, for his "podemos ya empezar" (447; "we can now begin," 424) is changed to "podemos empezar" (490; we can begin). Although the words appear as a memory, they are changed and become a part of José's consciousness and being. And even though the ending reproduces a modification of Licario's words to José, it is significant that *Paradiso* should close in the first-person plural, for in addition to synthesizing Licario's voice and José's memory, it suggests a merging of the autobiographical and fictive modes. It is interesting to speculate about the extent to which the ending represents a synthesis or meeting of the author/narrator and his hero. This brings into focus serious questions concerning writing, time, and identity. It is clear that if one considers identity as being centered exclusively in one entity and located only in one time and place, a meeting of the narrator and the hero is not possible. However, if one conceives of time, identity, and space as being fragmented or dispersed over continuums we do not fully understand, such a synthesis, or the beginning of such a synthesis, is possible in the synchronic world Lezama Lima has created. Chapters 12 and 13 center on the abolition of time and space, undoubtedly as a prelude to the novel's final chapter. These chapters also contain startling mergings of identities.

The closing chapter represents the authorial self's desire to merge with its own past in order to capture essences seemingly lost in time as well as its desire to find the rivers or ways that lead to paradise. The contradictions contained in these dialectics of time and identity are not alien to the novel, because the work's very title embodies this paradox, as it points simultaneously in two directions. The Eden suggested by the title refers to the lost security and essence of childhood and to a wish to be united with origins locked in the past. But it also points to the mythical promised land that is hidden somewhere in the misty shrouds of the future. In this respect, the novel's title captures the many dialectics of desire, particularly a longing for the past and a craving for the future. And poetry is the manifestation of this thirst for eternity, the wish to be free of time-bound limitations, the yearning for *Paradiso*.

6

Oppiano Licario and the Lost Center

Lezama Lima's religious faith and his intimate knowledge of a number of intellectual and spiritual traditions led him to conclude that the physical world is not the beginning and end of all things. He regarded the universe as a text to be deciphered, read, and interpreted. The poet's function, in his view, was to merge the visible and invisible realms, that is, to make known, by means of the poetic image, correspondences and relationships that are not readily apparent. He stated: "¿Qué es la sobrenaturaleza? La penetración de la imagen en la naturaleza engendra la sobrenaturaleza. En esa dimensión no me canso de repetir la frase de Pascal que fue una revelación para mí, 'como la verdadera naturaleza se ha perdido, todo puede ser naturaleza';la terrible fuerza afirmativa de esa frase, me decidió a colocar la imagen en el sitio de la naturaleza perdida, de esa manera frente al determinismo de la naturaleza, el hombre responde con el total arbitrio de la imagen. Y frente al pesimismo de la naturaleza perdida, la invencible alegría en el hombre de la imagen reconstruida"[1] (A68).

The affirmation of a poetic creed that is based in part on religious belief is present in his posthumous novel *Oppiano Licario*, but in this novel, faith is also accompanied by the darkening shadows of doubt and death. Many circumstances beyond his control prevented him from enjoying the fame that a lifelong devotion to letters had brought him. In addition, as he sensed that his life was drawing to a close, faith was continually threatened by the deterministic aspects of nature.

Like *Paradiso*, *Oppiano Licario* is based on a quest motif, with creativity playing a major role. José Cemí, the central character in both novels, moves toward self-identification and attempts

1. Lezama Lima, "Confluencias," in his *Las eras imaginarias*, 177–78.

to transform and overcome the world he lives in. In *Paradiso* the Eden-like existence of childhood is replaced by the trials of adolescence and young adulthood, but the work ends on a positive note with the suggestion that José will transcend the limitations of the world of experience. Although this theme continues in *Oppiano Licario,* it is not as convincingly presented; an ironic mode tends to undercut the affirmations the novel presents. Lezama Lima's search for liberation from the world of experience marks this novel as well, but it is tempered by a recognition that salvation depends on forces outside of human control—a realization that accompanied his growing awareness of the inability of human consciousness to overcome the negative forces of death. José ceases to be just an observer of life in *Oppiano Licario;* he participates in activities that symbolize the Fall.

Lezama Lima left the novel curiously incomplete, probably due to a combination of external and internal factors. There is no doubt that he was depressed during his last years and that he felt overwhelmed by the ascendent political ideology in Cuba, which he could not accept. But although Lezama Lima's personal situation was an important factor in his failure to complete *Oppiano Licario,* there are other possibilities that merit consideration. The novel's incompleteness could have been intentional; it conforms well with some of the thematic content. It is also possible that he could not reconcile the work's affirmations with the growing awareness that his own end was near. There are many contradictions in *Oppiano Licario,* and tension is generated within the text by meanings that move simultaneously in two directions.

Lezama Lima died on 9 August 1976, and *Oppiano Licario* was published the following year. Eloísa Lezama Lima has indicated that her brother frequently mentioned that the novel only lacked twenty or thirty pages, and that after his death, a diagram of the work was discovered in addition to the manuscript. She suggests that the cultural and political isolation that he endured during his last years might have been the cause of his failure to terminate the novel, citing a passage from *Oppiano Licario* that indicates his displeasure with the situation in

Cuba.[2] Lezama Lima's last years were not happy ones. Although he married María Luisa Bautista (a lifelong friend of his sister, Eloísa) after his mother's death in 1964, he found himself separated from family members who elected to live in exile as the revolution progressed. He also found himself in conflict with the regime because of his divergent views on the nature and purpose of art.[3] It was ironic and tragic that he was unable to fully enjoy the worldwide attention and fame he gained after the publication of *Paradiso* in 1966. His isolation was interrupted only by telephone conversations, letters, and occasional social calls from distinguished visitors such as Julio Cortázar.[4]

Lezama Lima's personal letters during this period reveal an aging and depressed man, who was accompanied only by his wife, was separated from his family, and rarely ventured into the world. The vitality of his personal cosmos depended on his imagination and on the echoes and memories of the past. Despite these difficulties, it is not surprising that he never left Cuba permanently; if he had elected to live in exile, it would have been an excruciating experience for him. Cuba in general and Havana in particular formed the center of his world, and it

2. Eloísa Lezama Lima, "Mi hermano," in José Lezama Lima, *Cartas*, 26. A description of an outline of the novel is contained in Enrico Mario Santí, "Hacia *Oppiano Licario*."

3. For personal accounts of Lezama Lima's difficulties with the government, see Herberto Padilla, "Lezama Lima frente a su discurso"; and Guillermo Cabrera Infante, "Vidas para leerlas."

4. In a letter to his sister dated August 1974, he wrote: "La universidad de la Aurora, en Cali, Colombia, me invitó al IV Congreso de la Narrativa Hispanoamericana, con tal de que diera una charla o una conferencia con otros dos escritores. Llegaron los pasajes aquí a La Habana, pero el resultado fue el de siempre: no se me concedió la salida. Ahora recibo otra invitación del Ateneo de Madrid, para dar unas conferencias. Siempre acepto, pero el resultado es previsible" (Lezama Lima, *Cartas*, 257). And in a letter dated September 1974: "Por la noche, María Luisa y yo leemos algún libro que nos gusta, como el maravilloso *Diario* de Paul Klee. Me parece que vivo esas existencias maravillosas, mientras permanezco, aunque con disgusto, inmovilizado, pues en el año pasado y en éste he recibido como seis invitaciones para viajar a España, a México, a Italia, a Colombia, y siempre con el mismo resultado. Me tengo que quedar en mi casita, hasta que Dios quiera. Estoy aburrido y cansado. Escribo, a veces, algún poemita y eso me tiene todavía en pie" (Ibid., 259). In a conversation in New York City on 28 December 1981, the organizer of the Cali conference, Gustavo Alvarez Gardeazábal, told me that at his request the Colombian Communist party had issued an invitation to Lezama Lima.

is hard to imagine him living apart from these sources of his identity. Because of the many references in his works to other cultures, critics occasionally claim that Lezama Lima's work is not Cuban. Such speculations are as devoid of validity in Lezama Lima's case as they are in those of Jorge Luis Borges and Octavio Paz, whose work has been accused of the same thing. The predominance of a cosmopolitan spirit does not necessarily mean that there is a denial or neglect of a national heritage; in fact, the opposite is true in the case of these three writers.

One of the major principles or figures that underlies both of Lezama Lima's novels is the search for absolutes or centers of meaning. This quest is frequently represented in various characters' pursuit of knowledge and an understanding of the world as well as in their awareness that there are hidden realities beyond the physical world. In *Paradiso* the investigation of family origins and José's movement toward creativity are important manifestations of this search. As José moves closer to a recognition of the need to embark on his own quest, the narration relies more heavily on ritualistic and mythic references. In *Oppiano Licario* it is Fronesis who undergoes this experience when, through the voice an an oracle, he gains an awareness of the unknown forces that are operating in the universe and humankind's obligation to participate in the celebration of these mysteries. But the revelation of absolutes is never complete, because they represent an unattainable goal. In existence before death, a sense of incompleteness is always present. In Lezama Lima's second novel, Licario refers to these truths when he describes his obsession with Etruscan culture as a search for lost essences.

> Por estos aires tenen que quedar vestigios de aquella ciencia, hoy desaparecida, de la ostentaria dedicada a estudiar las excepciones o prodigios que forman parte de la verdadera causalidad. Mi hermana y yo buscamos, quizá no lo encontremos nunca, el *nexus* de esos prodigios, lo que yo llamo las excepciones morfológicas que forman parte del rostro de lo invisible. Digo que quizás no lo encontraremos porque somos tan solo dueños de una mitad cada uno. Yo tengo la mitad que representa las coordenadas o fuerza asociativa de reminiscencia, ell la *visión* de reconstruir los fragmentos en un todo. Si yo lograra el *nexus* de la

> reminiscencia en el devenir y ella pudiera recordar en su totali-
> dad la fatalidad de cada movimiento, o la necesidad invariable de
> lo que sucede, lograríamos como una especie de esfera trans-
> parente, como un lapidario que hubiera encontrado una sustan-
> cia capaz de reproducir incesantemente el movimiento de los
> peces.[5] (A69)

The sense of incompleteness that is expressed in this passage
haunts many of the characters in both novels, and it is often
expressed by the quest for the center, which is evident in
Fronesis's search for his biological mother and in manifestations of erotic desire. Fronesis becomes the object of several
characters' yearnings because he represents what they do not
possess: serenity and stability. Fronesis is the object of two
violent attacks in *Oppiano Licario*, which suggests that the erotic
aspects of the quest for completeness contain many dangers.
In Lezama Lima's view, the search for unity leads many people
down false roads.

Licario uses the expression "morphological exceptions" in
the above quotation to refer to the links that lead to the revelation of the extraordinary and inexplicable. This expression is
indicative of his belief that the study of forms and structure can
reveal all-encompassing truth. The same words appear in the
title of an unpublished manuscript that his sister, Ynaca, passes on to José after Licario's death. The possession of the
manuscript is a grave responsibility, and Ynaca tells José: "No
tengo que subrayar que es para usted una responsibilidad
traágica la custodia de estos papeles" (137; A70). Ynaca's mention of "a tragic responsibility" has a prophetic ring. The
existence of the manuscript is a masterful narrative technique,
because the reader is curious about the contents and desires to
know what wisdom the manuscript contains.

When José returns home after receiving the manuscript, he
is too tired to read it. The next day he carefully puts it in a
wooden Chinese box and places the container in the middle of
a table in the center of his study. He then returns to Ynaca's
home, and they make love during a raging hurricane. When

5. Lezama Lima, *Oppiano Licario* (Mexico City: Ediciones Era, 1977), 171.
Subsequent quotations are from this edition and are noted in the text.

José returns home, he discovers that a dog has knocked open the box containing Licario's manuscript and that the pages have fallen into the floodwaters caused by the storm. "El agua había borrado la escritura, aunque al arrugarse el papel, le otorgaba como una pátina, como si al volatilizarse el carboncillo de la tinta quedase en la blancura de la página un texto indescifrable. Se acercó a la caja china y en un fondo precisó unas páginas donde aparecía un poema colocado entre la prosa, comenzó a besarla" (155; A71).

The poetic composition and traces of ink on white paper are all that is left of Licario's work. The poem, which consists of eight or more pages, was located "en medio del texto, ciñendo las dos partes como una bisagra" (140; in the middle of the text, binding the two parts like a hinge). Although the poem is all that remains of the manuscript, the reader never sees it because it is a part of *Oppiano Licario* that Lezama Lima never completed. Later in the novel, José sends a copy of the poem to Fronesis in a letter, but there is only a blank space in the text instead of the poem, along with a note from the publisher indicating that the poetic composition was not found in the original manuscript. Although José has lost Licario's work, he possesses the poem, and although the reader has the text of Lezama Lima's incomplete novel, he does not see the poetic composition. José and the reader are confronted by similar situations that are both marked by traces that indicate incompleteness and absence. This synthesis of presence and absence embodies much of the essence of Lezama Lima's art, because it marks the conjunction of tangible and intangible realms and operates as a sign of the necessity to search for secret and absent causes.

Oppiano Licario opens with an episode in which a young man is killed. After his death, his brother's emotional and psychological confusion is indicated by the statement: "La ausencia de lo real producía una presencia de lo irreal ofuscadora" (17; A72). The episodes involving death and the destroyed manuscript communicate a sense of loss, incompleteness, and absence, and both events are manifestations of one of the novel's most important themes—the search for the unknown and remote. These episodes symbolize the presence of the unknown in existence and the secrets of the cosmos. The disappearance of Licario's manuscript marks a loss of wisdom and knowledge; indeed it is indicated that the manuscript is sacred precisely because it is lost. In this regard, the awareness of an absence makes that which is absent valuable and creates the paradoxical sensation that it is present.

Later in the novel, an old woman who has the gift of prophecy tells Fronesis that it is his and José's destiny to reconstruct Licario's lost manuscript, and she predicts: "Lo que no pudieron alcanzar ni el tío Alberto, ni el Coronel, lo alcanzarán Cemí y tú" (209; A73). She is speaking of the quest for absolutes through creativity, and her declarations are one of many elements that link *Paradiso* and *Oppiano Licario*. The lost manuscript becomes a goal toward which the characters must move to fulfill their destiny, and the incompleteness of *Oppiano Licario* seems to invite the reader to undertake the same task. The wisdom of Lezama Lima's last novel is thus embodied in the work's unfinished configuration, because its incompleteness is a device that synthesizes form and content. The text confronts us with an absence and invites us to accept the responsibility of attempting to complete that which will always remain incomplete.

All of Lezama Lima's art is an invitation to participate in the quest for truth and to attempt to reveal the indecipherable, but it is the search rather than the attainment of this goal that is emphasized. In his view, life leads inevitably to death, but in the momentary escape from time that can be attained by the poetic image, we are offered glimpses of resurrection and eternity. According to Lezama Lima, imagery is the highest form of knowledge that humankind is capable of achieving, for it combines knowing with mystery and awe. The struggle that the quest for absolutes represents is embodied in the complexity of Lezama Lima's works, in that they resist interpretation, and their meanings are sometimes inaccessible. His interest in intricacy reflects his oft-stated belief that only the difficult is stimulating.

The unfinished state of *Oppiano Licario* conforms very well with the novel's thematic content. This affinity of form and content leads one to suspect that Lezama Lima must have concluded, at least on an intuitive level, that it was best to leave *Oppiano Licario* incomplete. Whether he intended to or not (and there is little in his writings that was not carefully thought out), Lezama Lima has extended a subtle invitation to his readers to participate in the quest that unified his life's work. And the incompleteness of the novel underscores a frequently used strategy in Lezama Lima's works: the avoidance of closure.

The lost manuscript and the poem the reader never sees are good examples of the expansive elements in *Oppiano Licario*. Their inaccessibility and importance stimulate one's imagination and provide speculation, particularly about the significance of absence. Within the context of the novel, the absence of Licario's text signifies more than the manuscript could have if it were present. In the larger context of both novels, the lost manuscript in *Oppiano Licario* complements and reverses the role played by chapter 12 in *Paradiso*. In *Paradiso* the text exists, but the identity and the intent of the narrator are uncertain, while in *Oppiano Licario* the author and the function of *Súmula, nunca infusa, de excepciones morfológicas* (ungiven compendium of morphological exceptions) are identified, but the text no longer exists. In both instances a decentralized entity is presented, and the reader's imagination must expand into the resulting vacuum. Lezama Lima uses an empty center in both novels to underscore his belief that there is a secret and privileged reference operating. In this regard, absence signifies presence.

José loses Licario's manuscript because he abandons the book during a hurricane in order to make love to Ynaca. His amorous encounter with Ynaca represents a gain, because a child is conceived, but the destruction of the manuscript is a profound loss. Ynaca's role in these events is shrouded in ambiguity. On one hand, it is she who delivers the manuscript to José, thereby giving him the opportunity to know Licario's most profound thoughts. But on the other hand, she is the temptress who causes José to abandon the manuscript when it is most in need of protection. Ynaca is thus a dual image that points simultaneously toward the pleasures of the flesh and toward the wisdom of the mind. There is an undercurrent of guilt in these events, because José's pursuit of worldly pleasure in his celebration of life with Ynaca removes him from the center of wisdom and spirituality that is represented by Licario's manuscript.

The misplacement of the manuscript and the ensuing sense of guilt are very suggestive in an autobiographical sense. In Lezama Lima's life, his parents, the family's social status, and his religious beliefs were centers of authority that he often idealized. The sense of loss and betrayal that José experiences in *Oppiano Licario* could be a reflection of the author's own feelings of unworthiness with regard to the authority figures he most respected. This explains, in part, the increasing presence of an ironic mode in Lezama Lima's works.

The quest motif in *Oppiano Licario* is frequently combined with a tragic sense of loss. In this sense, José's loss of the manuscript is symbolic of the Fall. José's actions can be interpreted as an allegory of the human condition, with its never-ending conflict between sexuality and spirituality. However, the manuscript is destined to be lost, because the wisdom it contains, if revealed, would cease to be secret. The importance of Licario's work is that it exemplifies the necessity of pursuing the mysterious and the obscure. For this reason, the narrator states: "Licario sabía que no había secretos, pero sabía también que había que buscar esos secretos" (145; A74).

Ynaca's husband is called "Abatón, el inaccesible" (177; Abatón, the inaccessible) because he is impotent; but her relationship with José is more fruitful. The passage that describes José and Ynaca's amorous meeting is one of the most poetic in the novel, and it contains many images and associations that remind the reader of episodes in *Paradiso*. José's movement toward Ynaca is a manifestation of the search for the mystic center. When he passes over the threshold of her home, he experiences the sensation of falling. "Al cerrarse las puertas nació en él una tensión, como si cayera al centro de las aguas, sintió un lince frente a las insinuaciones de la oscuridad. No era tan sólo el punto de la visibilidad que acrecía, era, por el contrario, como si toda su piel se pusiera en un aviso para recibir el pinchazo de una aguja. Esa tensión hacia un centro siguió en aumento al contemplar la escalera que nos llevaba a la biblioteca de Ynaca" (149; A75). The gravitation toward a center is combined with downward and upward movement (the references to falling and the staircase), and this combination of images that point simultaneously in two directions is indicative of Ynaca's conflicting influence on José's life. The contradiction is intensified by the references to "darkness" and "visibility" and by the subtle insertion of the autobiographical mode in the phrase, "the staircase that led us to Ynaca's library." These are additional examples of combinatory opposition—one of the fundamental strategies of Lezama Lima's writings.

There are many references in this episode that remind the reader of events in chapter 5 of *Paradiso*, particularly of Fibo's hurling of the compass against the blackboard. In both novels an intellectual environment—a school in *Paradiso* and a private library in *Oppiano Licario*—provides the setting for sexual activities. The result is an implied synthesis of thought and emotion. When Ynaca, in ritual preparation for the event that is about to take place, draws a circle, she is compared to a compass. "Ynaca con un pie como centro, como si fuese un compás, trazó un círculo" (150; A76). She burns José's clothing in the circle she has drawn. Although the reason for her actions is not at first clear, it becomes evident, through association based on contiguity, that it is an act of purification, in which she is attempting to ensure that their offspring will not be marked by the asthma that has always plagued José.

When Fibo throws the compass against the blackboard in *Paradiso*, he is venting his frustration, and the blackboard serves as a target for his rage. The library in Ynaca's home also contains a blackboard, which her husband normally uses. Abatón's relationship to the blackboard is similar to the teacher's in *Paradiso*. In both cases, the men are figures of sterility. In *Paradiso*, the instructor is a symbol of intellectual unproductiveness and boredom. This is suggested by the forms of the English verb *to freeze* that he writes on the blackboard. In *Oppiano Licario*, Abatón is a sign of sexual impotence.

As Ynaca and José make love, her sensations are projected

onto the blackboard. "Ante la penetración del aguijón creía proyectarse en la pizarra discos de colores, que primero abrían sus brazos, dilatando el color, hasta perderse en sus confines y luego, mientras cerraba los ojos en el éxtasis, se reducían a un punto, parecía que se extinguían, pero después girando con fuerza uniformemente acelerada, se iban desplegando espirales de colores, vibraciones, letras de alfabetos desconocidos, más rápidos en surgir que en sus agrupamientos o cadenetas significativas" (151; A77).

The circular and chromatic imagery intensifies and is combined with numbers as the discs vary in size and different colors appear. During the sexual act, Ynaca is identified with earth, and José, with solar energy. Their union is continually manifested in circle imagery. The maximum manifestation of the circle is the hurricane, with its rotary and sideways motions and its "eye" of absolute calm. The combination of these two movements and a calm center recalls José's sensations of falling and rising and the vertigo he experiences when he enters Ynaca's home. Passage through the eye of a hurricane is like passing through a void and into a realm of spacelessness and timelessness. For this reason, the blackboard, which is used as a focal point of all this energy and as an image of the void or of the storm's center, is described as being an extension of infinity. As in *Paradiso*, the blackboard is used as a spatial sign of the conjunction of great forces.

Lezama Lima clearly had the mythologies of the original inhabitants of Cuba in mind when he wrote this passage. They considered the hurricane a deity.[6] Given this connection, the linking of José with the storm recalls the significance of the Taino word that forms his surname. There are other associations that are derived from Cuba's past. For example, the word *manatee* appears as a substitution for *Ynaca*. José Juan Arrom has pointed out that the meaning of this word as used in *Paradiso* derives from its appearance in the chronicles of the discovery of the New World. "La imagen del manatí entra en las crónicas envuelta en un halo de lo asombroso, lo ilusorio y lo fantástico. El iniciador de esa corriente fue el propio Cristób-

6. Fernando Ortiz, *El huracán*.

al Colón. . . . Los manatíes que aparecen en las referidas páginas de *Paradiso* son, por consiguiente, metáforas que aluden a las 'sociables' sirenas que acompañan a Michelena en sus orgías"[7] (A78). It is clear that many of the same associations occur in *Oppiano Licario* when José abandons Licario's manuscript to experience the fabulous charms of the siren Ynaca. She offers a marvelous new world of erotic pleasure to José.

A number of substitutions in this scene are based on a metonymic chain that is associated with the sea. At one point, José's skin is described as "sweaty scales," and the lovers are referred to as "fish." The taste of salt as Ynaca savors her lover's body also links them to the sea. "Ynaca pasaba su rostro por todo el cuerpo de Cemí, sentía la sal de sus escamas sudorosas. Sentía como el sudor del diálogo amoroso nos convierte en peces. Ynaca restregaba su rostro en la humedad de la espalda de Cemí y saboreaba la sal como si chupara un pescado congelado" (154; A79). In another passage, man swims like a fish through a universe of language. "Manera de restituir, el hombre devuelve con su esperma y como un pez nada en el verbo universal" (153; A80). The process of creating metaphors that are based on an underlying metonymic chain is also evident in *Paradiso* and is indeed a fundamental aspect of Lezama Lima's art.

It has already been pointed out that circle imagery is used in *Paradiso* as a narrative strategy to unite diverse elements. There are also numerous references to the circle in *Oppiano Licario*, particularly in chapter 6, which includes the encounter between Ynaca and José and the destruction of Licario's manuscript. The frequent appearance of such references in these and other episodes in chapter 6 underscores the importance of this imagery in Lezama Lima's second novel. This chapter is a key section of the work, and it operates as a synthesis of the novel's main concerns. These central preoccupations include the search for a center, the many dichotomies of the human condition, and the significance of death.

7. Arrom, "Lo tradicional cubano en el mundo novelístico de José Lezama Lima," 472–73.

The concern with death is indicative of Lezama Lima's realization that his own demise was near at hand, and the pages of *Oppiano Licario* contain signs of a consciousness contemplating its own end. Licario's reappearance after his death is an affirmation of the possibility of resurrection and an assurance that his spiritual legacy is still a vital force. This assurance is particularly important because it affirms that an individual's influence can endure beyond the temporal limits of his life. Despite the intensity of Lezama Lima's religious faith, *Oppiano Licario* reflects a reluctance to abandon the self. Since all of Lezama Lima's works, both the poetry and the prose, are characterized by their self-referentiality, this is not surprising. This dilemma manifested itself in *Paradiso* particularly in the confrontation between autobiographical and fictive modes. Although the autobiographical is not as predominant in *Oppiano Licario*, there are indications of its presence in some startling shifts in narrative perspective, in philosophical observations on death, and in intertextual references to *Paradiso*.

Autobiographical elements are most noticeable in the passages that combine narrative fluctuations between the first and third persons with contemplations of the significance and meaning of death. This occurs in the following quotation.

> Una vez estábamos sentados en un parque, alguien pasó por el frente de nuestro banco tres o cuatro veces, se precipitó de pronto, tomó una máquina. Era Licario, que con un rasguño se apoderaba de la tarde. A medida que fue pasando el tiempo, Cemí se hizo hipersensible a esas llegadas de Licario. Aunque no fuese cierta la presencia de ese otro plano, de esa doble existencia, de esa desaparición, era una muestra de la complicadísima huella terrenal de Licario, pues muy pocos tienen fuerza reminiscente para poder crear en otra nueva perspectiva después de su muerte. Generalmente es un recuerdo muy atado, totalmente trágico, pero no como en el caso de Licario, infinitamente particularizado, universalmente mágico y abierto a las decisiones más inesperadas. Era un metáfora que en cualquier momento podía surgir, el infinito posible análogo de la metáfora, pues parecía que la muerte aumentaba más su posibilidad al actuar sobre una imagen extremadamente vigorosa e inesperada en el reino de lo incondicionado. (102; A81)

In this passage the confrontation with death is accompanied by a shift from an autobiographical to a fictive mode. The narrative begins in the first person plural but then shifts to José's perspective. This change is followed by observations on death that are related to the absence and presence of Licario. The narrative then moves to Licario's perspective, thus completing the attempt to overcome the limitations of life and death. This movement away from self-referential signs parallels the intensification of the paradoxical presence of an absence—the appearance of the dead Licario. On one hand, the self's diminishment seems to result in a glimpse of immortality. On the other, the shift away from self-referential signs can be regarded as an indirect expression of the self's desire that some type of existence will continue after death.

Lezama Lima's art is characterized by the uniqueness of his personal vision. Although the presence of the authorial self is sometimes overwhelming, at other times the unitary self dissolves and is replaced by a multiplicity. This artistic strategy is present in the frequent juxtaposition of autobiographical and fictive modes, in the fragmentation of the authorial self onto numerous characters, and in the displacement of sexual elements, particularly in *Paradiso*. The latter technique is used less frequently in *Oppiano Licario* as the vitality of life confronts the awesome specter of death, but this difference is counterbalanced by the intertextual network of associations that is created by the numerous references the narrator of *Oppiano Licario* makes to *Paradiso*.

So much has been made of Lezama Lima's Catholic background and religiosity that it has often been assumed that his work is primarily an extension into the contemporary era of long-established traditions. This has been particularly true of critics who rely heavily on Lezama Lima's essays to explicate his works and who therefore tend to see his creative endeavors as extensions of his essays or as manifestations of the philosophical systems therein. In reality Lezama Lima's outlook was ecumenical. He struggled to attain a total view of existence, and he tended to place individual tragedies within a cosmic view that strived for unity (a vision of existence as a divine comedy). He spent so much of his career imposing order on chaos that it is easy to overlook the dynamic disorder and fragmentation in his work. Lezama Lima was an assiduous if somewhat undisciplined reader of many writers and thinkers; along with Aquinas, Dante, and Góngora, he read Nietzsche, Joyce, and Heidegger. Within Cuban letters, he was influenced by the example of Enrique Labrador Ruiz's *El laberinto de sí mismo*[8]—by its fragmentation of form, its meditation on the creative process, and its subversion of conventionality in narrative fiction. There is much of the modern spirit in Lezama Lima's writings, and there are elements that tend to undermine or subvert the universal view he attempted to attain. The fragmentation of the self is certainly a crucial part of this contradictory tendency, for it challenges long-cherished notions of the unitary self and replaces the self with a plurality that is not always centered. Other subversive elements can be seen in the aspects of sexuality he has conveyed in his works and in the juxtaposition of pagan and Christian cultures throughout the text.

The search for the center is a persistent motif in Lezama Lima's work, but so is the elusiveness of this goal. His journey toward one principle or essence is never completed, because the end is only glimpsed and can therefore only be communicated in terms of absence. His work embodies the desire for unity and the search for a lost, unitary principle, but these are never permanently achievable realities. For Lezama Lima, the leap of faith required by his quest was couched in terms related to the commitment to creativity, and he emphasized the process rather than its goals. In this respect, the center is the commitment to creativity, but the perfection the writer seeks, which is symbolized by the circle, is never complete, because the circle never closes. This explains the incompleteness of *Oppiano Licario* and the termination of *Paradiso* just as José is initiated into adulthood and creativity. Lezama Lima frequently mentioned his intention to write a sequel to *Paradiso*, which was an indication of his desire to continue or finish the story he had started, but since the work depends on autobio-

8. Labrador Ruiz, *El laberinto de sí mismo* (Havana: Laberinto, 1933).

graphical sources, it could only be completed with the termination of its creator's existence. This situation is similar to that of Narcissus in Lezama Lima's first published poem, *Muerte de Narciso*, in which Narcissus contemplates his reflection in a river, knowing that his desire to unite himself with his image will result in his death.

The desire for the center is also contradictory because the center is a sign of death as well as of creativity. The poetic incarnation of the dead Colonel while the children are playing jacks in *Paradiso* and the appearance of José's deceased mentor in *Oppiano Licario* are examples of the merging of the center and death. The metonymical networks that extend throughout Lezama Lima's texts break down in the face of death, and the metaphorical apprehension of this dissolution is a manifestation of hope and emptiness. In such instances meaning moves in opposite ways at the same time, thereby creating contradictions, which are embodied in images that also point simultaneously in two directions. The abyss of death can only be answered with creativity. Lezama Lima's texts are attempts to fill the void, to stuff emptiness with the vigor of life, to challenge dissolution with the hermetic image. This leads to the conclusion that one of the main strategies of Lezama Lima's writings is the avoidance of closure. The emphasis on nonclosure can be seen in the absence of the manuscript in *Oppiano Licario*, in the incorporation of chapter 12 into *Paradiso*, and in Lezama Lima's general preference for the difficult.[9] This strategy allowed him to keep the vital questions open, the

9. Lezama Lima partially explained his interest in the challenge of the difficult in the opening paragraph of the essay "Mitos y cansancio clásico." His comments link artistic endeavors with a search for meaning in history:

Solo lo difícil es estimulante; sólo la resistencia que nos reta, es capaz de enarcar, suscitar y mantener nuestra potencia de conocimiento, pero en realidad ¿Qué es lo difícil? ¿lo sumergido, tan sólo, en las maternales aguas de lo oscuro? ¿lo originario sin causalidad, antítesis o logos? Es la forma en devenir en que un paisaje va hacia un sentido, una interpretación o una sencilla hermenéutica, para ir después hacia su reconstrucción que es en definitiva lo que marca su eficacia o desuso, su fuerza ordenancista o su apagado eco, que es su visión histórica. Una primera dificultad en su sentido; la otra, al mayor, la adquisición de una visión histórica. He ahí, pues la dificultad del sentido y de la visión histórica. Sentido o el encuentro de una causalidad regalada por las valoraciones

center moving, the circle incomplete.[10] Like the mule in Lezama Lima's great poem, "Rapsodia para el mulo," the reader of Lezama Lima's works traverses difficult paths, weighed down by the challenges of a complex work rather than by the burdens of life. Cinched by the text instead of by God, the reader slips between the words into the metaphorical abyss, but the downward fall is countered by the upward extension of hope.

In Lezama Lima's works, life is depicted as a paradox and as a meeting of contradictory forces. The intensification of faith that can be sensed in his last works was accompanied by increasing doubt as the cherished center became more decentralized and as the gravitation toward completeness was increasingly undermined by the lack of closure. More and more, his works became a dialogue with displacement, as the seeds of dissolution were seen in all things. In the final analysis, the displacement of life by death confirms an essentially entropic view of existence, which did not challenge or subvert his faith. It was the burden of the self and the fear of losing self-

---

> historicistas. Visión histórica, que es ese contrapunto o tejido entregado por la imago, por la imagen participando en la historia. (Lezama Lima, "Mitos y cansancio clásico," in his *La expresión americana* [Madrid: Alianza Editorial, 1969], 9–10)

10. Patricia Drechset Tobin has suggested that nonclosure represents a rebellion against the father.

> Mastery is the prerogative of the father, and in Western languages the unit of mastery is the sentence. In defining sentence mastery as a "cultural pleasure," Roland Barthes confirms the analogy between life and language, which I am defining as the genealogical imperative. For him, the locus is the sentence: "Linguistics has always believed in the sentence and the dignity of its predictive syntax, as the form of a logic, a rationality. The sentence is hierarchical: it implies subjections, subordinations, internal reactions. It is always obliged to end; in fact, it is the power of completion that defines sentence mastery. It is a *cultural* pleasure. The law of closure, a compulsive idealization, is intolerant of fragmentation and imperfection." The sentence, in other words, is a genealogy in miniature. At its origin it fathers a progeny of words, sustains them throughout in orderly descent and filial obedience, and through its act of closure maintains the family of words as an exclusive totality. (Tobin, *Time and the Novel*, 17–18)

Enrico Mario Santí focuses on textual "errors" in the novel and concludes: "La tradición como padre muere en la 'mala' escritura; el padre muere cuando se cita mal" (Santí, "Parridiso," 105).

referentiality that undermined his beliefs. His considerable aesthetic talents moved him simultaneously toward form and fragmentation as he searched for order in the violence of nature and in the chaos of history. In the process, he created works of permanent value that will constantly challenge our efforts to close circles of meaning. *Oppiano Licario* points simultaneously toward aperture and closure and toward dissolution and resolution. In this respect, the novel can be regarded as a metaphor of Lezama Lima's career and of his continual search for absolutes in a realm of limitations.

Appendix

Translations

Introduction

A1

Today, in Latin America and the Western world, the work of Lezama Lima has been recognized as one of the decisive of this century, and because of its quality and importance his name is now associated with that of Borges and Octavio Paz.

A2

Do not fall into the trap of criticism: a mimetic language, a recreation of the style that turns out to be a recreation of the author's "tics." Avoid any expression like Lezama's.

Chapter 1. The Poetic Vision

A3

"How certain the mule's step in the abyss.

Slow is the mule. He does not sense his mission.
His fate facing the stone, stone that bleeds
creating the open laughter of pomegranates.
His cracked skin, tiniest triumph now in the dark,
tiniest blind-winged clod.
The blindness, the glassiness, the water of your eyes
have the strength of a hidden tendon:
just so his motionless eyes scanning
the increasing fugitive dark.
The space of water between
his eyes and the open tunnel
fixes the centre that cinches him
like the necessary load of lead
to fall like the sound of the mule
falling in the abyss."

Lezama Lima, "Rhapsody for the Mule," trans. Donald Devenish Walsh, José Rodríguez Feo, and Dudley Fitts, in *Cuban Poetry 1959–1966*, ed. Claudia Beck and Sylvia Carranza, 121. Subsequent quotations are from this translation.

114

A4

"He has no power of creation or pursuit,
his eyes neither leap
nor seek the sanctuary sequestered
at earth's teeming border.
No creation; and is that perhaps
no feeling, no loving, no questioning?" (121)

A5

"His love for the four hoof-signs
in the ravine, the successive crests
of his glassy blind ascent,
the dark body swollen
by the water of origins,
not the water of redemption and perfume.
Each step is a step of the mule in the abyss." (122)

A6

"That steady step of the mule in the abyss
is often confused with sterility's painted gloves,
confused often with the first probings
of the dark denying head.
Confused through you, glassy outcast." (125)

A7

"Each step is a step, boxes of water, God-cinched,
trembling sleeps the powerful mule.
With his set and watery eyes
in each abyss the mule plants trees at last." (127)

A8

The mule's resistance sows in the abyss like poetic durability sows
resurging in the astral. One resists in the body and the other resists in
time, and one can see in both a fin searching for its unknown, known,
unknown complement.

A9

"How can we isolate the fragments of night
so as to grip something with our hands,
the way a hare penetrates the darkness
separating two stars
that lean on the glitter of the moist grass.
Night breathes in an untouchable moisture,
not in the center of the flying sphere,

and it ties up everything, corners or fragments,
until it weaves the unbreakable web of night,
subtle and whole, like the interlocking of your fingers,
barely letting the water pass through.
Like a magic basket
floating empty on the river."

Lezama Lima, "Fragments of the Night," trans. Orlando José Hernández, in *Review* 21–22 (Fall–Winter 1977): 39. Subsequent quotations are from this translation.

A10

"I wanted to rescue the fragments of night
And formed a universal substance;
then I started to dip
my fingers and eyes into the night,
I untied all the ropes anchoring the barge.
It was a struggle without end,
between what night would offer me
and what I wanted to wrest from night." (39–40)

A11

"As in a fire,
I wanted to salvage night's memories,
the clink into the interior of the checkmating move,
as when we knead dough for bread
with the palms of our hands.
Sleep again stopped the hare
scratching my arms
with turpentine sticks.
Laughing, it dealt out big scars on my face." (41)

A12

"I am waning,
I am a point that disappears and returns
and I fit completely into the *tokonoma*."

Lezama Lima, "The Pavilion of the Void," trans. Orlando José Hernández, in *Review* 21–22 (Fall–Winter 1977): 37. Subsequent quotations are from this translation.

A13

"Is the aridity within the void
the first and ultimate path?
I fall asleep, in the *tokonoma*
I evaporate the other who goes on walking." (37)

A14

In order to get to my novel, there was a need to write my essays and to write my poems. I said on several occasions that when I felt intelligible I wrote prose and when I felt obscure I wrote poetry. That is to say, the poetry is my obscure work and my absolutely certain work, searching for the center, the most meridian that could be shaped in my essays, has as a consequence the perspective of *Paradiso*.

Chapter 2. Metaphor and Metonymy in *Paradiso*

A15

Undoubtedly it is a poem-novel in the sense that it is removed from the habitual concept of what a novel is. *Paradiso* is based on metaphor, on the image; it is based on the negation of time, on the negation of accidents and in this sense its expressive devices are essentially almost poetic.

A16

"And from the distance of Aredo's Babylonian desk-seat he threw the compass at the black beach."

Lezama Lima, *Paradiso*, trans. Gregory Rabassa, 94. Subsequent translations are from this edition.

A17

"In the crisscrossing lead pipes, matching but irreconcilable, in the worn-out face of the shower, the bird of Angra Mainyu awakens like death." (91)

A18

"Olaya was nakedly asleep, his clothes swollen from lack of care, a castaway who has thrown his clothing in to feed the fire. His back was propped against the wall where the lead sternum of the shower grew. Between his index finger and the ring of his right hand, the flower of his sex was dangling in the ultimate boredom of nakedness, when sleep begins to make us nod in the first victory of Angra Mainyu, who awakens like death." (92–93)

A19

"Alberto was the first who showed surprise going into the classroom, the first who surprised and drank in the space that was slightly scratched by the new breathing that came to puncture it, to establish in one season its white coral reefs for those dermatite colonies of intertwined memories and flagella which discharged themselves through a mist that when pricked gave back its nettlesome rancors as an expression of protoplasmatic complements.

"When José Eugenio entered the classroom, in his first review of the mirroring and marvelous monster spread out within his reach, the figure least clear was that of the teacher. Amid the fog and foliage he saw a monster with tridents, polyhedrons that opened slightly, unfurling nervous flagella like a sea horse perched on the shell of a three-century-old turtle. And opposite was another monster, irreconcilable with the first, that surprised him with its fixed erection and the matutinal tegument of its skin. He began to penetrate into this monster of erection when the little director from inside his shell began to unmask himself, as if he were bringing out some gaudy pajamas for the malicious purpose of projecting his perversions and his monosyllables." (79)

A20

In this scene, which evokes as much as it describes, three figures are perceived by José Eugenio: the teacher, "the mirroring and marvelous monster" (79), and the "monster of erection" (79). In the pages that follow this passage, a transformation of the second figure occurs: "the mirroring and marvelous monster" in subsequent references is "the silvered surface of the whale calf" (80) and "the whale calf, the monster with silvery skin" (81). "Monster" is replaced by "whale calf," and then the two terms appear together. "Mirroring" becomes "silvered surface" and "silvery skin." The two lines of associations then merge in "the soft corpulence of Enrique Aredo, the milky provocation of his skin" (81).

A21

"But very soon the silvered surface of the whale calf would be scratched by an elastic caterpillar." (80)

A22

The metonymic chain of sea-related associations is the basis for many metaphoric substitutions. Some examples, including a few that have already been mentioned, are: "whale calf" (80) for student, "the softest sand dunes of the body" (80) for buttocks, "the whale calf, the monster with silvery skin" (81) for a student who is the object of Fibo's aggressive stabs, "the jubilation of dogfish when they surround a Homeric salmon" (83) for student athletes swarming around a ball, "a squid's ink" (87) for inkwell, "like the emptiness a squid sucks to produce an exceptional, albino ink" (91) for soapsuds going down a shower drain, and "black beach" (94) for blackboard. A further extension of this chain exists in the sentence preceding the appearance of "black beach." The compass that is hurled against the blackboard is described as being the size of a "blind crab." After sinking into the blackboard, it makes a sound like that of a crab chewing on a palm leaf.

A23

"On that first day of school José Eugenio was going to begin the contemplation of evil in its pure gratuitousness; the first demonstration that he would see, beyond the conciliar difficulty of the *quod erat demonstrandum* of the incontrovertible existence of original sin in every creature." (80)

A24

"With the point of the compass, he pounded ferociously on the door of the dungeon, but inside the box he found only cigarette butts. He tried to destroy the essential symmetry with his voracious shoes, a paper-crushing zigzag burial mound on top of the ashes.

"These were what remained of the darkly conjured daughter of Inachus, the maddened Io, caught between the memory of the showers' music and the cigarettes stamped on by Cuevarolliot's fury, the remains of an Argos whose flight none had been able to impede. But the small one pinioned there, conversant with the resentful love of the daughter of Inachus, had taken possession of the first day on which his ransomed fire would burn." (94)

The Rabassa version translates "fuego rescatado" as "ransomed fire," but I prefer "rescued fire."

A25

"A firefly basking in the music of the darkness made corporeal. When Alberto Olaya reached the corner by the school, he held his newly lit cigarette like a trumpet." (94)

A26

"The storyteller's mermaid came out jingling her rings of keys. She was a crippled girl who limped about on a rickety wooden skeleton. She leaned against the door, and her lone leg, covered with a flesh-colored stocking, had the look of a mermaid's tail recumbent on a muddy sand spit. She sang. Olaya entered the bower clinging to the defender of the cactus flower, fear visibly overshadowing the secret chill of pleasure. The muddy mermaid's song was sinking with the ring of keys. As they came out, the memory of the mermaid made them both gulp, but they swore that they both would set a foot on her." (101)

A27

"filled a place in the family imagination which had the same terrible extension as those frosty Christmas Eves in Jacksonville." (61–62)

A28

"something of an ancient sacrifice about it. Except that the Colonel did not know to which deity he was making the offering." (131)

A29

"He smoothed out the wrinkles in his shirt, feeling his respiratory contractions begin as his hostile deity, asthma, landed on his chest like a giant fly and began to flail around, laughing and swiftly growing so fat that Cemí could not support it long enough to shoo it away." (147)

The Rabassa version translates "enemiga divinidad" as "hostile deity," but I prefer "divine enemy."

Chapter 3. The Paradigm of Characterization

A30

I cannot consider myself, I have never considered myself, a novelist. Poetry has always been my form of expression: but the moment arrived in which I saw that there was something else in a poem, that a poem was being formed into a novel, that there were characters that functioned in life like metaphors, like images; I saw how they became intertwined, how they merged, how they changed and then I realized that a poem could extend itself into a novel and that in reality every great novel was a great poem.

A31

"Fifty years after his death, Uncle Alberto's rage rose up again on the rebound when compared to that of the Duke of Provence, whose fury consisted in breaking the royal china service, piece by piece." (77)

A32

"He remembered that they also said his father appeared at night in Morro Castle, in the pavilion where he had taught his class, a man who fulfilled his sense of duty even in death." (240)

A33

"It appeared that his destiny was to enrich their happy unity and prolong that instant given us to contemplate integrity and harmony." (31)

A34

"José Eugenio expanded his thirty-year-old chest. He seemed to be smoking the sea breeze. He widened his nostrils, drank in an epic quantity of oxygen, and then let it out through his mouth with slow puffs. The peace and innocent color of the waters awakened a shouting pride in him, one that was natural and savage. Standing in front of him he saw his five-year-old son, skinny, his ribs showing, panting as the breeze grew stronger, and then trembling as he tried to hide it, slyly watching his father as he pretended to breathe normally." (127)

A35

"The thirty-three years of his life were of a merry severity; he seemed to be driving his wife and three children along the rough and roadless places of his own resolute blood, where everything was gained through happiness, clarity, and secret strength. A melon under his arm was the explosive symbol of one of his round and full days." (14)

A36

"To the four jacks players, the tiles were an oscillating crystal that broke up silently after coming together silently, never losing its tremor, making way for fragments of military cloth, feeling harsh hobnails, freshly polished buttons. The fragments disappeared, reappearing at once, joined to new and larger pieces, the buttons falling into their sequence. The collar of the tunic was precisely starched, waiting for the face that would complete it. Rialta, peacefully hallucinated, went on playing jacks, getting close to twelve, the way one climbs up a staircase half-asleep, carrying a glass of water with such assurance that the water in it does not move. The rim of the circle was hardening until it began to look like incandescent metal. Suddenly, in a flash, the cloud broke up to make way for a new vision. On the tiles imprisoned by the circle the full tunic of the Colonel appeared, a darkish yellow that grew lighter, the buttons on the four pockets brighter than copper." (161)

A37

"For the family dynasty of the Cemís and the Olayas, the small diabolic dose of Alberto was more than enough." (166)

A38

"the archetype of elegant manhood, the chosen one, the daring one, gallant, disdainful." (168)

A39

"when Alberto's in a calm mood, he has a joy that gives us all strength." (177)

A40

"The smoke surrounds him like a suit of armor, its burnished metal bound with the sea's congealed mist." (71)

A41

"lighted his cigarette and let out a presumptuous puff of smoke." (103)

A42

"He had been sitting in his study for a long time, watching the lighted tips of his cigarettes parade by like shots at a target. He looked at the sparks but didn't stir them, so that frequently the matches burned his fingers, while the glow dimmed by the long ashes finally extinguished itself in the alliance of the saliva's moisture and the invading embers.

"The exercise of poetry, the verbal search for unknown finality, developed in him a strange perspicacity for words which acquire an animistic relief when grouped in space, seated like sibyls at an assembly of spirits." (355)

The Rabassa version translates "cigarros" as "cigarettes," but I believe "cigars" is more accurate.

A43

"Come close so you can hear what your Uncle Alberto wrote, and you'll get acquainted with him and his special ebullience. This is the first time you'll hear language made into nature, with all its artifices of allusions and loving pedantry." (169)

A44

"Something fundamental had happened and reached him. As if he had been struck by a harpoon of clarity, the family idea of Alberto's demonism finally struck him and wiped him out." (171)

A45

"Everything your father couldn't do, you will, over the years; such terrible misfortune cannot come to a family without filling such emptiness with a strange meaning, without that absence returning for its ransom." (227)

A46

"Don't reject danger and always try what is most difficult. There's a danger that confronts us in the form of substitution, there's also a danger that sick people seek out, a sterile danger, the danger without epiphany. But when a man throughout his days has tested what is most difficult, he knows that he has lived in danger, and even though its existence has been silent, even though the succession of its waves has been peaceful, he knows that a day has been assigned to him in which he will be transfigured, and he will not see the fish inside the current but the fish in the starry basket of eternity." (228)

Chapter 4. Organizational Configurations: Plot and Fabula

A47

"The wax of the face and hands epitomized what he, because of what she said and because he had never seen a wax piece like that before, thought was real death. That it wasn't even an image, but a very ordinary wax mold made with no excess of realism, added to the confusion, and Cemí, six years old, could not perceive the objects he was discovering, as he lacked the framework that might have helped him to form analogies and group dissimilar objects around nuclei to be distributed and newly arranged." (141–42)

A48

"The orderly drew back the sheet. Suddenly Cemí saw his father dead, in his dress uniform now, his arms folded across his chest. The skin did not resemble the wax that he saw in his nightmares, St. Flora's waxen face that had brought him his first memory of death. He waited for a moment, his father seemed motionless. He did not disintegrate, as his grandmother said had happened to her father when he was exhumed. The skin no longer had blood coursing through it, but it was not St. Flora's wax of death. It was not the whirlwind of dust from his grandmother's tale. Yet there was his father, dead. The orderly covered him with the sheet again." (156)

A49

"That brought him to meditate on the manner in which those spatial rearrangements were produced in him, that ordering of the invisible, that feeling for stalactites. He was able to establish that those groupings had temporal roots, had nothing to do with spatial groupings, which are always a still life; for the viewer, the flow of time converted those spatial cities into figures, through which time, as it passed back and forth like the labor of the tides on the coral reefs, produced a kind of eternal change of the figures, which by being situated in the distance were a permanent embryo." (358)

The Rabassa version translates "eterno retorno" as "eternal change," but I believe "eternal return" is more accurate.

A50

"The next day, when he reached Upsalón in the morning, Cemí noticed in all the groups a festivity, almost a stir, which interrupted the classes. The mocking gravity of the god Terminus seemed to be at the root of those groups. A single theme brought on remarks that were rich, pseudo-scientific, libertine, or disapproving. At the center, the god Terminus, his jawbone moving with a laugh celebrating this single theme in song, with an enormous phallus and a horn in his right hand. Each time his jaw moved up and down, there was a corresponding rhythmic movement of the hand with the horn that covered the hymn-like length of the phallus.

"The remarks cheered all the groups in their nascent sperm. One narrator, and afterwards the variants and inventive games. Cemí recalled his vision of the day before, at the fortress of La Fuerza; that was the kind that made him laugh, when he had mounted dolphins on horses whose mutations ran from the inorganic world to tetanus. Dolphins, symbols of sexual deviation, gamboling beside the shell where the Cyprian goddess wraps herself in veils of salt spray." (241)

A51

Memory is the soul's plasma, it is always creative, seminal, since we remember from the root of the species.

A52

The novel is about a life, José Cemí's and mine, which is embedded in every one of its recesses.

A53

"Now the critic can perceive the drops of the temporal, but not as other mortals do, for death, not sleep, begins now to really give him the eternal, in which time cannot be conquered, beginning with the nonexistence of that sin which is time." (404)

A54

"Cemí forged ahead into the thickening night, feeling that it was becoming more and more difficult to penetrate it." (460)

Chapter 5. The Autobiographical Paradox

A55

"As they passed by a tomb in which the body of St. Flora was reproduced in wax, Doña Augusta said to her grandson: 'That's a saint there, a real saint.' The wax of the face and hands epitomized what I, because of what my grandmother said and because I had never seen a real saint before, thought was real death."

This is my translation. The Rabassa version changes the *I* to *he*, which greatly modifies the meaning.

A56

"Some doubters will think that I never said these words, that you invented them, but when you give the answer and the testimony, you and I will know that I did say them and that I will say them as long as I live and that you will continue saying them after I have died." (228)

A57

"I know that those are the most beautiful words Cemí ever heard in his life after the ones he read in the Gospels and that he will never hear any others that will so decisively set him in motion, but so many things had happened that day that he began to feel the nervous indecision that precedes the bronchial whistle of an asthmatic crisis." (228)

A58

"Another phrase that had that kind of druidic overtone, the most untouchable family distance where faces faded away as if seen under the sea . . . was that word 'hearer' heard and savored by José Cemí as the impossible key to an unknown world." (44)

A59

"That visibility of absence, that dominion of absence, was Cemí's strongest trait. In him what wasn't there, was; the invisible occupied the first plane in the visible, converting itself into a visible with dizzying possibilities; absence was presence, penetration." (328)

A60

has in its center the notion of salvation and it finds as a way to salvation poetic creation. Those who forget that Lezama is Catholic, forget that he is a Catholic poet and that that is the only way it is possible to deeply understand his system. That is why the novel is called *Paradiso*, and not only as a superficial homage to the other great

Catholic poet. Lezama's man, banished from the paradise of infancy, lost in the world, saves himself through poetry. Against Heidegger's affirmation that man is destined for death, Lezama raises his profound conviction that man is destined for resurrection, and that resurrection arrives by means of poetry.

A61

The sister Ynaca Eco Licario appears rendering the poetical decree of a promised land.

A62

After his imprisonment, Martí must have felt like he was being reborn again in an image of resurrection, just as after his death he resurges again in the flesh. The barrenness of the desert and his new symbolic appearance in exile balance one another, and because of that in *Paradiso*, in order to propitiate the last encounter of José Cemí with Oppiano Licario, in order to reach a new coincidence, the Tibetan city, he has to cross all the occurrences and recurrences of the night. The placental descent of the nocturnal, the abiter at midnight, appear like a variant of the desert and exile; all the possibilities of the poetical system have been put in motion, so that Cemí can attend his meeting with Licario.

A63

"He remembered Doña Augusta's tale, his dead great-grandfather in a dress uniform, intact, who had suddenly, like an invisible whirlwind, broken up into colored dust. The wax of St. Flora's face and hands, inside the glass casket, offering a resistant death, hard as the image of the evaporated body. The wax suddenly ready for the sleigh of touch, offering an infinite sliding. Suddenly his father, hidden behind a column and telling him in a disguised voice: 'When we were alive we walked one route, and now that we're dead we walk a different route.' The phrase 'walk a different route' became alive for him. The image of Oppiano Licaro rose up, but now he was alone in the bus with all the other seats empty, tinkling his coin collection, ordering the little horses on his Greek drachmas to stop, their chests and haunches disproportionate in relation to their faces and the small legs pacing on top of a drum. The immense drum of the night, a silent drum that fabricated absences, hollows, withdrawals, fragments into which an arm of the sea made its way." (464)

A64

"Like her brother she showed a completely religious self-confidence: her self was formed by two intersecting lines. Their point of intersection was the coincidence of her chance and her destiny." (464)

A65

"Like a magic mirror it caught the radiation of ideas, the column of self-destruction of knowledge rose up with the flame's slenderness, was reflected in the mirror, and left its mark. It was the tail of Juno, the starry sky that was reflected in the parenthesis of the constellation." (465)

A66

"I don't call him, because he comes,
like two stars that cross
in their exalted laws,
he knows their elliptical orbit.   4

I was, but he will be,
when I am pure knowledge,
the stone brought on the wind,
he will wrap me in Egyptian linen.   8

Reason and memory by chance
will see the dove attain
faith in the super-natural.   11

The spider and the image in place of body
cannot be, I am not dead.   13

I saw your father die; and now, Cemí, stumble." (465)   14

A67

Once more he heard: rhythm of hesychasts, we can begin.

This is my translation. The Rabassa version (466) includes the word "now," which does not appear in the Spanish version of this passage.

Chapter 6. *Oppiano Licario* and the Lost Center

A68

What is afterlife? The penetration of imagery in nature engenders afterlife. To that extent I never tire of repeating Pascal's statement which was a revelation for me, "since true nature has been lost, all can be nature." The terrible affirmative force of that statement moved me to place imagery within the context of lost nature, in this way in the face of the determinism of nature; man responds with the total arbitrariness of imagery. And faced with the pessimism of lost nature, [one sees] man's invincible joy in the reconstructed image.

A69

There must remain in this environment vestiges of that science, now lost, of ostentatiousness dedicated to the study of the exceptions or marvels that form part of true causality. My sister and I are searching for perhaps we will never find, the *nexus* of those wonders, what I call the morphological exceptions which form part of the face of the invisible. I say that perhaps we may never find it because each one of us represents only a half of the whole. Mine is the half that represents the coordinates or associative power of reminiscence, her's the *vision* to reconstruct fragments into a whole. If I should achieve the *nexus* of reminiscence in becoming and if she could remember in its totality the destiny of each movement, or the invariable necessity of whatever happens, we would prevail like a type of transparent sphere, like a lapidary that would have found the substance capable of reproducing incessantly the movement of fish.

A70

"I don't have to emphasize that the custody of these papers is a tragic responsibility for you."

A71

The water had erased the writing, although as the paper crumpled it seemed to have a patina, as if there remained on the whiteness of the page an indecipherable text as the black traces of the ink vaporized. He approached the Chinese box and in the bottom of one of its compartments he made out some pages where a poem appeared among the prose, he began to kiss it.

A72

The absence of the real produced a presence of dazzling irreality.

A73

"What neither Uncle Alberto nor the Colonel could accomplish, you and Cemí will achieve."

A74

Licario knew there were no secrets, but he also knew that one had to search for those secrets.

A75

As the doors closed a tension blossomed in him as if he were falling into the center of the sea, and he sensed a lynx within the insinuations of the darkness. It wasn't only the point of visibility that was increasing, it was, on the contrary, as if all his skin was expecting to receive a needle's prick. This tension that gravitated toward a center continued growing as we contemplated the staircase that led us to Ynaca's library.

A76

Ynaca with a foot as a center, as if she were a compass, drew a circle.

A77

As the barb penetrated she was conscious of colored disks being projected onto the blackboard, which first opened their arms, dilating the color, until they were lost within their confines and then, while she closed her eyes in ecstasy, they were reduced to a point, it seemed they were extinguishing themselves, but after spinning with a uniformly accelerating force, spirals of colors proceeded to unfold, along with vibrations and letters of unknown alphabets, bursting forth more rapidly than they could form into groups or patterns.

A78

The image of the manatee appears in the chronicles shrouded in a halo of the astonishing, the illusory and the fantastic. The initiator of this tendency was Christopher Columbus. . . . The manatees that appeared in the mentioned pages of *Paradiso* are, consequently, metaphors that allude to the "sociable" sirens that accompany Michelena in his orgies.

A79

Ynaca nuzzled her face all over all of Cemí's body, she felt the salt of his sweaty scales. She sensed how the sweat of carnal dialogue converts us into fish. Ynaca forced her face into the moisture of Cemí's back and savored the salt as if she were sucking a frozen fish.

A80

As a form of restitution, man gives something back through his sperm and like a fish, swims in the universal Word.

A81

Once we were seated in a park, someone passed in front of our bench three or four times, suddenly rushed off, and got into a car. It was Licario who with a flourish took over the afternoon. As time passed, Cemí became hypersensitive to those arrivals of Licario.

Although the presence of that other space, of that duplicate existence, of that disappearance wasn't certain, it was an indication of the very complicated, earthly presence of Licario, as very few after their death have the reminiscent force to create in another a new perspective. Generally, it is a very restrained, totally tragic memory, but not in the case of Licario, infinitely particularized, universally magic and open to the most unexpected decisions. It was a metaphor that in any moment could appear, the infinite possible analogy of metaphor, for it seemed that in the realm of the absolute, death increased its possibility of acting on an extremely vigorous and unexpected image.

Bibliography

There are a number of fine bibliographies on Lezama Lima, which are listed below. Justo C. Ulloa's bibliography, which contains over six hundred entries, is the most inclusive. Since some of these bibliographies are very thorough and are readily available in this country, I have limited the list of Lezama Lima's writings to his books (except in the case of the translations) and of the critical studies to works that are cited in the text, recent items that do not appear in the bibliographies, and studies that were particularly helpful to me. Some of Lezama Lima's works have appeared in print several times, and although the titles may be the same, variations in content sometimes exist, particularly in the essays. For example, the 1970 edition of *La cantidad hechizada* contains more works than the 1974 edition.

I. Works of Lezama Lima (listed chronologically by genre)

1. Fiction

Paradiso. Havana: Ediciones Unión, 1966.
———. Buenos Aires: Ediciones de la Flor, 1968.
———. Prologue by Julio Ramón Ribeyro. 2 vols. Lima: Ediciones Paradiso, 1968.
———. Revised by the author and edited by Julio Cortázar and Carlos Monsiváis. Mexico City: Ediciones Era, 1968.
———. Madrid: Editorial Fundamentos, 1974.
———. Annotations, critical essays, and bibliography by Eloísa Lezama Lima. Madrid: Ediciones Cátedra, 1980.
Cangrejos y golondrinas. Buenos Aires: Editorial Calicanto, 1977. Short stories and essays.
Oppiano Licario. Mexico City: Ediciones Era, 1977.
———. Havana: Editorial Arte y Literatura, 1977.
Juego de las decapitaciones. Prologue by José Angel Valente. Barcelona: Montesinos, 1982. Short stories.

2. Poetry

Muerte de Narciso. Havana: Úcar, García y Cía., 1937.
Enemigo rumor. Havana: Ediciones Espuela de Plata, 1941.

———. Havana: Úcar, García y Cía., 1941.

Aventuras sigilosas. Havana: Editorial Orígenes, 1945.

La fijeza. Havana: Editorial Orígenes, 1949.

Dador. Havana: Úcar, García y Cía., 1960.

Nuevo encuentro con Victor Manuel. Diseño de Fayad Jamis. Havana: Biblioteca Nacional José Martí, 1970. I have not seen this eight-page publication, which is indexed under poetry in *Bibliografía cubana, 1971* (Havana: Biblioteca Nacional José Martí, 1973), but it is most likely the work of the same title that appeared in *Fragmentos a su imán*.

Fragmentos a su imán. Prologue by Cintio Vitier. Havana: Editorial Arte y Literatura, 1977.

———. Introductory poem by Octavio Paz. Mexico City: Ediciones Era, 1978.

———. Prologues by José Agustín Goytisolo and Cintio Vitier. Barcelona: Lumen, 1978.

3. Essays

La pintura de Arístides Fernández. Havana: Ministerio de Educación, 1950.

Analecta del reloj. Havana: Editorial Orígenes, 1953.

La expresión americana. Havana: Instituto Nacional de Cultura, 1957.

———. Madrid: Alianza Editorial, 1969.

———. Santiago, Chile: Editorial Universitaria, 1969.

Tratados en La Habana. Havana: Úcar, García for the Universidad Central de Las Villas, 1958.

———. Buenos Aires: Ediciones de la Flor, 1969.

———. Santiago, Chile: Editorial Orbe, 1970.

La expresión americana y otros ensayos. Montevideo: Arca, 1969.

La cantidad hechizada. Havana: UNEAC, 1970.

———. Madrid: Júcar, 1974.

Esferaimagen. Sierpe de Don Luis de Góngora. Las imagenes posibles. Introductory poems by José Agustín Goytisolo and Herberto Padilla. Barcelona: Tusquets, 1970.

Algunos tratados en La Habana. Barcelona: Editorial Anagrama, 1971.

Las eras imaginarias. Madrid: Editorial Fundamentos, 1971.

Introducción a los vasos órficos. Barcelona: Barral Editores, 1971.

4. Interviews

Coloquio con Juan Ramón Jiménez. Havana: Publicaciones de la Secretaría de Educación, 1938.

5. *Collections*

Poesía completa. Havana: Instituto del Libro, 1970. Does not include *Fragmentos a su imán*.

———. Barcelona: Barral Editores, 1975. Does not include *Fragmentos a su imán*.

Obras completas. Vol. 1. Introduction by Cintio Vitier. Mexico City: Aguilar, 1975.

Obras completas. Vol. 2. Mexico City: Aguilar, 1977. These volumes do not contain *Fragmentos a su imán* and *Oppiano Licario*.

6. *Documents*

Cartas (1939–1976). Selection, prologue, and notes by Eloísa Lezama Lima. Madrid: Editorial Orígenes, 1979.

7. *Translations*

Fitts, Dudley, ed. *Anthology of Contemporary Latin American Poetry*. Norfolk, Conn.: A New Directions Book, 1947. Includes: "Rhapsody for the Mule," translated by Donald Devenish Walsh, José Rodríguez Feo, and Dudley Fitts.

Beck, Claudia, and Sylvia Carranza, eds. *Cuban Poetry 1959–1966*. Havana: Book Institute, 1967. Includes: "Ode to Julián del Cassal," translated by Claudia Beck; and "Rhapsody for the Mule," translated by Donald Devenish Walsh, José Rodríguez Feo, and Dudley Fitts.

Donoso, José, and William Henkin, eds. *The TriQuarterly Anthology of Contemporary Latin American Literature*. New York: E. P. Dutton, 1969. Includes: "Boredom of the Second Day," "Calm," "The Cords," "Now Has No Weight," and "Song of Lost Paradise," translated by Elinor Randall.

Mundus Artium 2:1 (Winter 1969). Includes: "An Obscure Meadow Lures Me," and "Summons of the Desirer," translated by Nathaniel Tarn.

Tarn, Nathaniel, ed. *Con Cuba. An Anthology of Cuban Poetry of the Last Sixty Years*. London: Cape Goliard Press, 1969. Includes: "An Obscure Meadow Lures Me," "Tell Me, Ask Me," and "Summons of the Desirer," translated by Nathaniel Tarn.

Caracciolo Trejo, Enrique, ed. *The Penguin Book of Latin American Verse*. Baltimore: Penguin Books, 1971. Includes: "Cry of the Wishful Man," "Fragments" (excerpt), "The First Bower of Friendship" (excerpt), and "Nocturnal Fish," translated by John Hill.

Carpentier, Hortense, and Janet Brof, eds. *Doors and Mirrors: Fiction and Poetry from Spanish American (1920–1970).* New York: The Viking Press, 1972. Includes: *Paradiso* (selection), translated by Tim Reynolds.

Paradiso. Translated by Gregory Rabassa. New York: Farrar, Straus & Giroux, 1974.

Review, nos. 21–22 (Fall–Winter 1977). Includes: "Ah, That You Escape," "Fragments of Night," "The Gods," and "The Pavilion of the Void," translated by Orlando José Hernández.

Rodríguez Monegal, Emir, ed. *The Borzoi Anthology of Latin American Literature.* Vol. 2. New York: Alfred A. Knopf, 1977. Includes: *Paradiso* (excerpt), translated by Gregory Rabassa; "Boredom of the Second Day," "The Cords," and "Now Has No Weight," translated by Elinor Randall; and "An Obscure Meadow Lures Me," and "Summons of the Desirer," translated by Nathaniel Tarn.

Armand, Octavio, ed. *Toward an Image of Latin American Poetry.* Durango, Colo.: Logbride-Rhodes, 1982. Includes: "A Bridge, A Great Bridge," "Call of the Desirous," "A Dark Meadow Invites Me," "Death of Time," "The Fragments of the Night," "Ah, That You Escape," and "Weight of Taste," translated by Willis Barnstone.

II. Bibliographies

Fazzolari, Margarita Junco. "Bibliografía." In *'Paradiso' y el sistema poético de Lezama Lima,* 163–78. Buenos Aires: Fernando García Gambeiro, 1979.

Flores, Angel. *Bibliografía de escritores hispanoamericanos / A Bibliography of Spanish American Writers, 1609–1974,* 246–48. New York: Gordian Press, 1975.

Foster, David W. "A Bibliography of the Fiction of Carpentier, Cabrera Infante, and Lezama Lima: Works and Criticism." *Abraxas* 1, no. 3 (Spring 1971): 305–10.

Lezama Lima, Eloísa. "Bibliografía." In *Paradiso,* by José Lezama Lima, 97–105. Madrid: Ediciones Cátedra, 1980.

Peavler, Terry J. "Prose Fiction, Criticism and Theory in Cuban Journals: An Annotated Bibliography." *Cuban Studies / Estudios Cubanos* 7, no. 1 (January 1977): 58–118.

Simón Martínez, Pedro. "Bibliografía." In his *Recopilación de textos sobre José Lezama Lima,* 345–75. Havana: Casa de las Américas, 1970. Lezama Lima's works compiled by Araceli García-Carranza.

Ulloa, Justo C. "Contribución a la bibliografía de y sobre José Lezama Lima." In his *José Lezama Lima: textos críticos,* 119–56. Miami: Ediciones Universal, 1979.

III. Criticism and History

Alvarez Bravo, Armando, ed. *Orbita de Lezama Lima.* Havana: Colección Orbita, 1966.

Anderson-Imbert, Enrique. *Métodos de crítica literaria.* Madrid: Revista de Occidente, 1969.

Arrom, José Juan. *Mitología y artes prehispánicas en las Antillas.* Mexico City: Editorial Siglo XXI, 1975.

———. "Lo tradicional cubano en el mundo novelístico de José Lezama Lima." *Revista Iberoamericana* 41, nos. 92–93 (July–December 1975): 469–77.

Bejel, Emilio. "La dialéctica del deseo en *Aventuras sigilosas* de Lezama Lima." *Texto Crítico* 5, no. 13 (April–June 1979): 135–45.

———. "Lezama o las equiprobabilidades del olvido." In *José Lezama Lima: textos críticos,* edited by Justo C. Ulloa, 22–38. Miami: Ediciones Universal, 1979.

Brushwood, John S. *Genteel Barbarism: Experiments in Analysis of Nineteenth-Century Spanish-American Novels.* Lincoln: University of Nebraska Press, 1981.

Cabrera Infante, Guillermo. "Encuentros y recuerdos con José Lezama Lima." *Vuelta* 1, no. 3 (1977): 46–48.

———. "Vidas para leerlas." *Vuelta* 4, no. 41 (April 1980): 4–16.

Cascardi, Anthony J. "Reference in Lezama Lima's *Muerte de Narciso.*" *Journal of Spanish Studies: Twentieth Century* 5, no. 11 (Spring 1977): 5–11.

Chiampi Cortez, Irlemar. "La proliferación barroca en *Paradiso.*" In *José Lezama Lima: textos críticos,* edited by Justo C. Ulloa, 82–90. Miami: Ediciones Universal, 1979.

Cortázar, Julio. "Para llegar a Lezama Lima." *Unión* 5, no. 4 (October–December 1966): 36–60. Also in his *La vuelta al día en ochenta mundos,* 135–55. Mexico City: Editorial Siglo XXI, 1967.

Diccionario de la literatura cubana. Havana: Editorial Letras Cubanas, 1980.

Echavarren, Roberto. "Obertura de *Paradiso.*" *Eco* 202 (August 1978): 1043–75.

Eliason, Norman E. *Tarheel Talk.* Chapel Hill: University of North Carolina Press, 1956.

Farmer, John S., and W. E. Henley, eds. *Slang and its Analogues*. London: Harrison & Son, 1893.

Fazzolari, Margarita Junco. *'Paradiso' y el sistema poético de Lezama Lima*. Buenos Aires: Fernando García Gambeiro, 1979.

———. "Reader's Guide to *Paradiso*." *Review* 29, no. 1 (May–August 1981): 47–54.

Fernández Moreno, César, ed. *America Latina en su literatura*. Mexico City: Editorial Siglo XXI, 1977.

Fernández Retamar, Roberto. *La poesía contemporánea en Cuba (1927–1953)*. Havana: Editorial Orígenes, 1954.

Forastieri Braschi, Eduardo. "Nota al 'aspa volteando incesante oscuro.' " *Río Piedras* (University of Puerto Rico), no. 2 (March 1973): 137–41.

Foster, David William. *Studies in the Contemporary Spanish-American Short Story*. Columbia: University of Missouri Press, 1979.

García Vega, Lorenzo. *Los años de orígenes*. Caracas: Monte Avila, 1979.

González Echevarría, Roberto. "Apetitos de Góngora y Lezama." *Revista Iberoamericana* 41, no. 93 (July–December 1975): 479–91. Also in his *Relecturas: estudios de literatura cubana*, 95–118. Caracas: Monte Avila, 1976.

Gimbernat de González, Ester. "*Paradiso*: reino de la poesía." *Perspectives on Contemporary Literature* 5 (1979): 116–23.

———. "La transgresión, regla del juego en la novelística de José Lezama Lima." In *Latin American Fiction Today*, edited by Rose S. Minc, 147–52. Takoma Park, Md.: Ediciones Hispamérica, 1980.

———. "La vuelta de Oppiano Licario." *Eco* 222 (April 1980): 648–64.

Goytisolo, José Agustín. "La espiral milagrosa." In *Fragmentos a su imán*, by José Lezama Lima, 7–21. Barcelona: Lumen, 1978.

Henríquez Ureña, Max. *Panorama histórico de la literatura cubana*. 2 vols. Puerto Rico: Ediciones Mirador, 1963.

Jiménez Eman, Gabriel. "La imagen para mí es la vida." *Imagen* 109 (December 1976): 42–46. This interview was also published in *Talud* (Mérida, Venezuela) 4, nos. 7–8 (May 1975).

Lavín Cerda, Hernán. "José Lezama Lima o la agonía verbal." *Texto Crítico* 5, no. 13 (April–June 1979): 126–34.

Lezama Lima, Eloísa. "*Fragmentos a su imán*: últimos poemas de José Lezama Lima." *Consenso* 2, no. 4 (November 1978): 21–23.

———. "Mi hermano." In *José Lezama Lima: textos críticos*, edited by Justo C. Ulloa, 11–17. Miami: Ediciones Universal, 1979. An amplified version is in *Cartas (1939–1976)*, by José Lezama Lima, 11–40. Madrid: Editorial Orígenes, 1979.

———. "*Paradiso:* novela poema." In *Paradiso,* by José Lezama Lima, 47–94. Madrid: Ediciones Cátedra, 1980.

———. "Para leer *Paradiso.*" In *Paradiso,* by José Lezama Lima, 13–15. Madrid: Ediciones Cátedra, 1980.

———. "Un sistema poético del universo." In *Paradiso,* by José Lezama Lima, 31–46. Madrid: Ediciones Cátedra, 1980.

———. "Vida, pasión y creación de José Lezama Lima: fechas claves para una cronología." In *Paradiso,* by José Lezama Lima, 16–30. Madrid: Ediciones Cátedra, 1980.

Lihn, Enrique. "*Paradiso,* novela y homosexualidad," *Hispamérica* 8, no. 22 (1979): 3–21.

Lutz, Robyn Rothrock. "The Poetry of José Lezama Lima." Ph.D. diss., University of Kansas, 1980.

———. "The Tribute to Everyday Reality in José Lezama Lima's *Fragmentos a su imán.*" *Journal of Spanish Studies: Twentieth Century* 8, no. 2 (Winter 1980): 249–66.

Marinello, Juan. *Literatura hispanoamericana; hombres, meditaciones.* Mexico City: Ediciones de la Universidad Nacional de México, 1937.

———. *Orbita de Juan Marinello.* Selection and notes by Angel Augier. Havana: Colección Orbita, 1968.

Martínez Laínez, Fernando. *Palabra cubana.* Madrid: Akal Editor, 1975.

Matamoro, Blas. "*Oppiano Licario:* seis modelos en busca de una síntesis." *Texto Crítico* 5, no. 13 (April–June 1979): 112–25.

Mathews, Mitford M. *A Dictionary of Americanisms on Historic Principles.* Chicago: University of Chicago Press, 1966.

Menton, Seymour. *Prose Fiction of the Cuban Revolution.* Austin: University of Texas Press, 1975.

Mignolo, Walter. "*Paradiso:* derivación y red." *Texto Crítico* 5, no. 13 (April–June 1979): 90–111.

Ortega, Julio. "*La expresión americana:* una teoría de la cultura." *Eco* 187 (May 1977): 55–63. Also in *José Lezama Lima: textos críticos,* edited by Justo C. Ulloa, 66–74. Miami: Ediciones Universal, 1979.

Ortiz, Fernando. *Contrapunto cubano del tabaco y el azúcar.* Havana: Jesús Montero, 1940.

———. *Las cuatro culturas indias de Cuba.* Havana: Arellano y Cía., 1943.

———. *Los factores humanos de la cubanidad.* Havana: Molina y Cía., 1940.

———. *El huracán: su mitología y sus símbolos.* Mexico City: Fondo de Cultura Económica, 1947.

Padilla, Herberto. "Lezama Lima frente a su discurso." *Linden Lane Magazine* 1, no. 1 (January–March 1982): 16–18.

Pellón, Gustavo. *"Paradiso,* un fibroma de diecisiete libras." *Hispamérica* 9, no. 25–26 (August 1980): 147–51.

Persin, Margo. "Language as Form and Content in *Paradiso." The American Hispanist* 1, no. 8 (April 1976): 11–16.

Prieto, Abel E. "Poesía póstuma de José Lezama Lima." *Casa de las Américas* 19, no. 112 (January–February 1979): 143–49.

Ríos-Avila, Rubén. "The Origin and the Island: Lezama and Mallarmé." *Latin American Literary Review* 8, no. 16 (Spring–Summer 1980): 242–55.

Rodríguez Monegal, Emir. "La nueva novela vista desde Cuba." *Revista Iberoamericana* 41, nos. 91–93 (July–December 1975): 647–62.

———. *"Paradiso:* una silogística del sobresalto." *Revista Iberoamericana* 41, no. 91–93 (July–December 1975): 523–33.

———. *"Paradiso* en su contexto." *Mundo Nuevo* 24 (June 1968): 40–44. Also in *Imagen* 25 (May 1968): 15–30; *Review* (Fall 1974): 30–34; Rodríguez Monegal, *Narradores de esta América,* 130–55. 2d ed. Montevideo: Editorial Alfa, 1974.

———, ed. *The Borzoi Anthology of Latin American Literature.* Vol. 2. New York: Alfred A. Knopf, 1977.

Ruiz Barrionuevo, Carmen. *El 'Paradiso' de Lezama Lima.* Madrid: Insula, 1980.

Santí, Enrico Mario. "Hacia *Oppiano Licario." Revista Iberoamericana* 47, nos. 116–17 (July–December 1981): 273–79.

———. "Parridiso." In *José Lezama Lima: textos críticos,* edited by Justo C. Ulloa, 91–114. Miami: Ediciones Universal, 1979. Also in *Modern Language Notes* 94, no. 2 (March 1979): 343–65.

Sarduy, Severo. "Dispersión (Falsas notas / Homenaje a Lezama)." In his *Escrito sobre un cuerpo,* 61–89. Buenos Aires: Editorial Sudamericana, 1969. Also in *Mundo Nuevo* 24 (June 1968): 5–17.

———. *"Oppiano Licario* de José Lezama Lima." *Vuelta* 2, no. 18 (May 1978): 31–35.

Simón Martínez, Pedro, ed. *Recopilación de textos sobre José Lezama Lima.* Havana: Casa de las Américas, 1970.

Souza, Raymond D. "La dinámica de la caracterización en *Paradiso."* In *José Lezama Lima: textos críticos,* edited by Justo C. Ulloa, 75–81. Miami: Ediciones Universal, 1979.

———. "La imagen del círculo en *Paradiso* de Lezama Lima." *Caribe* 2, no. 2 (Fall 1977): 29–35.

———. *Major Cuban Novelists: Innovation and Tradition.* Columbia: University of Missouri Press, 1976.

———. "Die Sinneswelt Lezama Limas." In *Aspekte von José Lezama Lima 'Paradiso,'* edited by Mechtild Strausfeld, 59–85. Frankfurt: Suhrkamp Verlag, 1979.

Sucre, Guillermo. "Lezama Lima: el logos de la imaginación." *Eco* 29, no. 175 (March 1975): 9–38. Also in his *La máscara, la transparencia,* 181–206, Caracas: Monte Avila, 1975; and in *Revista Iberoamericana* 41, nos. 92–93 (July–December 1975): 493–508.

Suetonius Tranquillus, Gaius. *The Lives of the Caesars.* Introduction, translation, and commentary by George W. Mooney. London: Longmans, Green & Co., 1930.

Ulloa, Justo C., ed. *José Lezama Lima: textos críticos.* Miami: Ediciones Universal, 1979.

Alvarez de Ulloa, Leonor. "Ordenamiento secreto de la poética de Lezama." In *José Lezama Lima: textos críticos,* edited by Justo C. Ulloa, 38–65. Miami: Ediciones Universal, 1979.

Valdivieso, Jaime. *Bajo el signo de Orfeo: Lezama Lima y Proust.* Madrid: Editorial Orígenes, 1980.

Vitier, Cintio. *Lo cubano en la poesía.* Havana: Úcar, García for the Universidad Central de las Villas, 1958.

———. "Nueva lectura de Lezama." In *Fragmentos a su imán,* by José Lezama Lima. Havana: Editorial Arte y Literatura, 1977; and Barcelona: Lumen, 1978, 23–36.

———. "La obra de José Lezama Lima." In *Obras completas,* by José Lezama Lima, 1:11–64. Mexico City: Aguilar, 1975.

Xirau, Ramón. *Poesía y conocimiento: Borges, Lezama Lima, Octavio Paz.* Mexico City: Joaquín Mortiz, 1978.

Yurkievich, Saúl. *La confabulación con la palabra.* Madrid: Taurus, 1978.

IV. Theory

Bakhtin, M. M., and P. N. Medvedev. *The Formal Method in Literary Scholarship.* Translated by Albert J. Wehrle. Baltimore: Johns Hopkins University Press, 1978.

Barthes, Roland. *Elements of Semiology.* Translated by Annette Lavers and Colin Smith. New York: Hill & Wang, 1977.

———. *S/Z.* Translated by Richard Miller. New York: Hill & Wang, 1974.

———. "Textual Analysis of a Tale by Edgar Poe." Translated by Donald G. Marshall. *Poe Studies* 10, no. 1 (June 1977): 1–12.

——. *Writing Degree Zero.* Translated by Annette Lavers and Colin Smith. New York: Hill & Wang, 1979.

Blanchard, Marc Eli. *Description: Sign, Self, Desire: Critical Theory in the Wake of Semiotics.* The Hague: Mouton, 1980.

Bray, Frank Chapin. *Bray's University Dictionary of Mythology.* New York: Apollo Editions, 1964.

Bremond, Claude. *Logique du récit.* Paris: Seuil, 1973.

Brooks, Cleanth, and Robert Penn Warren. *Understanding Fiction.* New York: Appleton-Century-Crofts, 1959.

Brushwood, John S. "Sobre el referente y la transformación narrativa." *Semiosis* 6 (January–June 1981): 39–55.

Campbell, Joseph. *The Hero with a Thousand Faces.* New York: Pantheon Books, 1949.

——. *The Masks of God: Creative Mythology.* New York: Penguin Books, 1978.

Champagne, Roland A. "Semiotic Directions for Modern Fiction." *Dispositio* 3, nos. 7–8 (Spring–Summer 1978): 85–102.

Chatman, Seymour. *Story and Discourse: Narrative Structure in Fiction and Film.* Ithaca, N.Y.: Cornell University Press, 1980.

Cirlot, Juan Eduardo. *A Dictionary of Symbols.* Translated by Jack Sage. New York: Philosophical Library, 1962.

Culler, Jonathan. *The Pursuit of Signs: Semiotics, Literature, Deconstruction.* Ithaca, N.Y.: Cornell University Press, 1981.

——. *Structuralist Poetics.* Ithaca, N.Y.: Cornell University Press, 1975.

DeGeorge, Fernande M. "From Russian Formalism to French Structuralism." *Comparative Literature Studies* 14, no. 1 (March 1977): 20–29.

DeGeorge, Richard, and Fernande DeGeorge, eds. *The Structuralists from Marx to Lévi-Strauss.* Garden City, N.Y.: Anchor Books, 1972.

Derrida, Jacques. *Of Grammatology.* Translated by Gayatri Chakravorty Spivak. Baltimore: Johns Hopkins University Press, 1976.

——. *Spurs: Nietzsche's Styles.* Translated by Barbara Harlow. Chicago: University of Chicago Press, 1976.

——. *Writing and Difference.* Translated by Alan Bass. Chicago: University of Chicago Press, 1978.

Ducrot, Oswald, and Tzvetan Todorov. *Diccionario enciclopédico de las ciencias del lenguaje.* Translated by Enrique Pezzoni. Mexico City: Editorial Siglo XXI, 1974.

Eco, Umberto. *The Role of the Reader: Explorations in the Semiotics of Texts.* Bloomington: Indiana University Press, 1979.

———. *A Theory of Semiotics*. Bloomington: Indiana University Press, 1976.

Erlich, Victor. *Russian Formalism: History–Doctrine*. 2d ed. The Hague: Mouton, 1955.

Fowler, Roger. *Linguistics and the Novel*. London: Methuen and Co., 1977.

García Berrio, Antonio. *Significado actual del formalismo ruso*. Barcelona: Editorial Planeta, 1973.

Genette, Gérard. *Figures*. Paris: Seuil, 1966.

———. *Figures II*. Paris: Seuil, 1969.

———. *Figures III*. Paris: Seuil, 1972.

———. *Narrative Discourse: An Essay in Method*. Translated by Jane E. Lewin. Ithaca, N.Y.: Cornell University Press, 1980.

Grimes, Joseph E. *The Thread of Discourse*. The Hague: Mouton, 1974.

Guirand, Felix, ed. *New Larousse Encyclopedia of Mythology*. Translated by Richard Aldington and Delano Ames. New York: Hamlyn Publishing Group, 1974.

Halliday, M. A. K., and Ruqaiya Hasan. *Cohesion in English*. London: Longman, 1976.

Hawkes, Terence. *Structuralism and Semiotics*. Berkeley and Los Angeles: University of California Press, 1977.

Hegel, Georg Wilhelm Friedrich. *The Philosophy of History*. Translated by J. Sibree. New York: Dover Publications, 1956.

Iser, Wolfgang. *The Act of Reading: A Theory of Aesthetic Response*. Baltimore: Johns Hopkins University Press, 1980.

Jakobson, Roman. "Closing Statement: Linguistics and Poetics." In *Style in Language*, edited by Thomas A. Sebeok, 350–77. Cambridge: MIT Press, 1960.

Jakobson, Roman, and Morris Halle. *Fundamentals of Language*. The Hague: Mouton, 1956.

Jung, Carl G. *The Portable Jung*. Edited by Joseph Campbell and translated by R. F. C. Hull. New York: Penguin Books, 1981.

Kaster, Joseph. *Putnam's Concise Mythological Dictionary*. New York: Capricorn Books, 1964.

Kinneavy, James L. *A Theory of Discourse*. Englewood Cliffs, N.J.: Prentice-Hall, 1971.

Krieger, Murray. "Literature vs. Ecriture: Constructions and Deconstructions in Recent Critical Theory." *Studies in the Literary Imagination* 12, no. 1 (Spring 1979): 1–17.

Kristeva, Julia. *Desire in Language: A Semiotic Approach to Literature and Art*. Translated by Thomas Gora and Alice Jardine. New York: Columbia University Press, 1980.

Lacan, Jacques. *Ecrits: A Selection*. Translated by Alan Sheridan. New York: Norton, 1977.

Lakoff, George, and Mark Johnson. *Metaphors We Live By*. Chicago: University of Chicago Press, 1980.

Le Guern, Michel. *La metáfora y la metonimia*. Translated by Augusto de Gálvez-Cañero y Pidal. Madrid: Ediciones Cátedra, 1980.

Leitch, Vincent B. "The Book of Deconstructive Criticism." *Studies in the Literary Imagination* 12, no. 1 (Spring 1979): 19–39.

———. "A Primer of Recent Critical Theories." *College English* 39, no. 2 (October 1977): 139–52.

Lemon, Lee T., and Marion J. Reis, eds. and trans. *Russian Formalist Criticism: Four Essays*. Lincoln: University of Nebraska Press, 1965.

Lévi-Strauss, Claude. *Myth and Meaning*. New York: Schocken Books, 1979.

Lewis, Thomas E. "Notes toward a Theory of the Referent," *PMLA* 94, no. 3 (May 1979): 459–75.

Lyons, John. *Semantics*. 2 vols. Cambridge: Cambridge University Press, 1977.

Matejka, Ladislav, and Krystyna Pomorska, eds. *Readings in Russian Poetics: Formalist and Structuralist Views*. Cambridge: MIT Press, 1971.

Mehlman, Jeffrey. *A Structural Study of Autobiography: Proust, Leiris, Sartre, Lévi-Strauss*. Ithaca, N.Y.: Cornell University Press, 1974.

Merrell, Floyd. "Metaphor and Metonymy: A Key to Narrative Structure." *Language and Style* 11, no. 3 (1978): 146–59.

———. "Structuralism and Beyond: A Critique of Presuppositions." *Diógenes* 92 (1975): 67–103.

Mitchell, W. J. T., ed. *On Narrative*. Chicago: University of Chicago Press, 1981.

Olney, James, ed. *Autobiography: Essays Theoretical and Critical*. Princeton, N.J.: Princeton University Press, 1980.

———. *Metaphors of the Self*. Princeton, N.J.: Princeton University Press, 1972.

Piaget, Jean. *Structuralism*. Translated by Chaninah Maschler. New York: Basic Books, 1970.

Prada Oropeza, Renato. *La autonomía literaria*. Jalapa, Mexico: Universidad Veracruzana, 1977.

———, ed. *Lingüística y literatura*. Jalapa, Mexico: Universidad Veracruzana, 1978.

Pratt, Mary Louise. *Toward a Speech Act Theory of Literary Discourse*. Bloomington: Indiana University Press, 1977.

Propp, Vladimir I. *Morphology of the Folktale.* Translated by Laurence Scott. Austin: University of Texas Press, 1958.

Ricoeur, Paul. *The Rule of Metaphor.* Translated by Robert Czerny, Kathleen McLaughlin, and John Costello, S.J. Toronto: University of Toronto Press, 1981.

Riffaterre, Michael. *Semiotics of Poetry.* Bloomington: Indiana University Press, 1978.

Ruegg, Maria. "Metaphor and Metonymy: The Logic of Structuralist Rhetoric." In *Glyph 6,* edited by Rodolphe Gasché, Carol Jacobs, and Henry Sussman, 141–57. Baltimore: Johns Hopkins University Press, 1979.

Scholes, Robert. *Structuralism in Literature: An Introduction.* New Haven: Yale University Press, 1974.

———. "Toward a Semiotics of Literature." *Critical Inquiry* 4, no. 1 (Autumn 1977): 105–20.

Scholes, Robert, and Robert Kellogg. *The Nature of Narrative.* Oxford: Oxford University Press, 1966.

Segre, Cesare. *Semiotics and Literary Criticism.* Translated by John Meddemmen. The Hague: Mouton, 1973.

———. *Structures and Time: Narration, Poetry, Models.* Translated by John Meddemmen. Chicago: University of Chicago Press, 1979.

Selz, Dorothy B. "Structuralism for the Non-Specialist: A Glossary and a Bibliography." *College English* 37, no. 2 (October 1975): 160–66.

Seung, T. K. *Structuralism and Hermeneutics.* New York: Columbia University Press, 1982.

Spengemann, William C. *The Forms of Autobiography: Episodes in the History of a Literary Genre.* New Haven: Yale University Press, 1980.

Sternberg, Meir. *Expositional Modes and Temporal Ordering in Fiction.* Baltimore: Johns Hopkins University Press, 1978.

Sturrock, John, ed. *Structuralism and Since: From Lévi-Strauss to Derrida.* Oxford: Oxford University Press, 1979.

Suleiman, Susan R., and Inge Crosman, eds. *The Reader in the Text: Essays on Audience and Interpretation.* Princeton, N.J.: Princeton University Press, 1980.

Surmelian, Leon. *Techniques of Fiction Writing: Measure and Madness.* Garden City, N.Y.: Doubleday, 1968.

Tobin, Patricia Drechset. *Time and the Novel: The Genealogical Imperative.* Princeton, N.J.: Princeton University Press, 1978.

Todorov, Tzvetan. *Introduction to Poetics.* Translated by Richard Howard. Minneapolis: University of Minnesota Press, 1981.

————. *The Poetics of Prose.* Translated by Richard Howard. Ithaca, N.Y.: Cornell University Press, 1977.

————, ed. *Teoría de la literatura de los formalistas rusos.* Translated by Ana María Nethol. Buenos Aires: Editorial Siglo XXI, 1976.

Watt, Ian. *The Rise of the Novel.* Berkeley and Los Angeles: University of California Press, 1957.

Wellek, René. *Concepts of Criticism.* New Haven: Yale University Press, 1971.

Wellek, René, and Austin Warren. *Theory of Literature.* 3d ed. New York: Harcourt, Brace & World, 1956.

White, Hayden. *Metahistory: The Historical Imagination in Nineteenth-Century Europe.* Baltimore: Johns Hopkins University Press, 1973.

————. *Tropics of Discourse: Essays in Cultural Criticism.* Baltimore: Johns Hopkins University Press, 1978.

Index